BRONTËS WERE HERE

REFLECTIONS ON THE FAMILY'S LIFE & TRAVELS

BY WILLIAM CLARKE

1977
E. J. Morten (Publishers)
Didsbury, Manchester

First published 1977
by
E. J. Morten, Publishers
A division of
Eric J. Morten (Booksellers) Ltd.
6 Warburton Street
Didsbury, Manchester 20.

© William Clarke, 1977

ISBN 0 85972 037 3

Set by Print Co-ordination, Macclesfield.
Printed and bound in Great Britain by
Redwood Burn Limited, Trowbridge & Esher

CONTENTS

FOREWORD

The intelligent reader, confronted with this particular piece of work, may well exclaim — "Oh no . . . not another book on the Brontes!"

Let it be said, of course. Of the making of books on this remarkable family there would seem to be no end. And not only books. There have been at least a couple of plays, to the best of my knowledge. Nor have I yet forgotten the excellent television series on the same subject.

As for the novels, thousands (maybe millions) of people who have never read them have nevertheless been enthralled by the number of screen versions made of both 'Jane Eyre' and 'Wuthering Heights'. 'Villette' and 'The Tenant of Wildfell Hall' have also been lavishly produced on TV, though I have yet to see an equivalent production of either 'Agnes Grey' or 'Shirley'.

Truly there is no way of getting away from the Brontes.

What then is my excuse for attempting yet another volume on the same subject?

Well, for one thing, I make no claim to have written an authoritative biography. Nor can this book be described as either scholarly or critical in its approach. Such books are all too readily available to the knowledgeable student who will very soon find that he has bitten off a great deal more than he can possibly chew in one lifetime.

I cannot lay claim to have re-examined all those documents, manuscripts and letters scattered about in libraries, museums, and colleges both in this country and abroad. They have already been over-exposed by investigators before me. There is nothing more to be squeezed out of them. Certainly nothing new.

Somewhere or other, perhaps, some further addition to the writings of the Bronte sisters may still be waiting discovery . . . new letters, new poems — even (dare one hope?) that new novel of Emily's which she would appear to have promised her publishers. I am getting a little too old now to be exploring dusty attics and cupboards in whatever places the Brontes managed temporarily to settle. I can only hope that someone younger, and a great deal more fortunate may one day unearth treasure of that kind. And, indeed, it is possible. Quite recently a photograph of Haworth churchyard has come to light which lays claim to include Charlotte, Emily, Anne, Branwell, Mr Nicholls and Ellen Nussey posed, primly, among the upright and flattened tombstones. It may well be authentic though I prefer to keep an open mind on the subject. I am a realist in such matters and indeed my whole approach has been such in writing this book. I have had in mind those possible readers who know little or nothing about the Brontes, their friends and acquaintances. For that reason I have tried to make the following account of them as light and entertaining and as free from erudition as will bear continued scrutiny.

I started out knowing little about the Brontes myself. I ended up a raving enthusiast. To attain that blissful state of mind I got away as far as possible from the study and th cloister with the aid of maps and a stout pair of walking shoes. That I necessarily soaked myself in everything appertaining to the subject on my return goes without saying. How else would I have retained my ardour and (hopefully) that of my readers?

This book is therefore as much a topographical as a biographical guide. It will have proved successful only if I have been able to convert at least one reader to follow in my footsteps.

Cliftonville,   William Clarke
Kent
November, 1976

Chapter 1

EMDALE, CO. DOWN (1777 - 1802)

I FIRST SAW the Rev. Patrick Bronte's birthplace in 1934.
I was on the road from Belfast to Newry and happened to
stop over for a drink and a snack in Banbridge. There I got
into conversation with a Catholic priest named Father
O'Reilly who, observing how absorbed I was in the first
few pages of a pocket edition of Wuthering Heights,
reckoned rightly that I was by way of being a friend of the
family.

"Did you know Emily's father worked here in
Banbridge once?" he enquired. "For a linen-draper, I
believe. Of course he was only a lad then."

I knew very little about the Brontes in fact, being only
a lad myself, but I couldn't help being interested. "Yes, he
was born not all that far from here," my informant continued. "Place called Emdale, just off the main road on the
way to Rathfriland."

It transpired that Father O'Reilly was very conveniently
en route to Dublin where he gave me to understand he was
taking over the running of a back-street boys' club. I was
half-hiking, half-hitchhiking, myself, and he had a car,
though admittedly a bit of an old banger. He volunteered
to drop me off in Newry where my intention was to spend
a few days with a maiden aunt. "I'll show you Patrick's
birthplace," he said. "You're not likely to forget it in a
hurry, though you may well want to."

I didn't know what he meant at the time but was only
too glad to accept the offer of a lift. We left Banbridge
behind us and after bumping along for some four or five
miles arrived at a village called Loughbrickland, a picturesque little place in a delightful country setting. From
there we turned off the main road and proceeded for
about the same distance in the direction of Rathfriland.

This was the Vale of Emdale, Father O'Reilly informed me and when I remarked how high the hills were in the background he looked quite shocked. "Those are the Mountains of Mourne," he said. "The ones that in the song 'run down to the Sea'."

And this," he exclaimed a moment or two after, "is Patrick Bronte's birthplace! I'll pull in the car and you can hop out and take a look."

☆ ☆ ☆ ☆

I really thought he was joking at first and more particularly because he didn't offer to come with me. It was no more than a cairn, a heap of stones, half-roofed over with some kind of thatch that reminded me of a mattress left out in the rain.

There was no misinterpreting my disappointment, but Father O'Reilly made no comment till I was back in the car and its bonnet was pointed the way we had come. "It never was much more than that," he observed, coolly. "Just a two-roomed stone cottage, a wayside shack really. I doubt if you could have swung a cat round in it properly, always assuming you had reached the stage where you felt you had to."

"And Patrick Bronte was born *there* . . ?" I was so shaken I could only whisper my incredulity. Father O'Reilly was obviously enjoying my discomfiture. "The first of ten children," he said. "Five boys and five girls. They called him Patrick because he was born on St. Patrick's Day, 1777."

This was too much even for me to swallow. "You said yourself you could hardly swing a cat round . . ." I began. In trying to slap me on the back, from sheer appreciation of the joke, Father O'Reilly nearly had us both in a ditch. "Oh, Good Lord no . . ." he chuckled. "The family had moved on a bit in more ways than one before they began to increase to that extent. They ended up down in Ballynaskeagh, as a matter of fact. Quite a roomy mansion by all accounts, and well they needed it by then."

On the main road to Newry again from Loughbrickland,

a distance of about twelve miles, my companion filled me in on most of the details. Patrick's father, he said, was a Protestant, and his mother was a Roman Catholic, and though such marriages didn't work out well as a rule this one seems to have come off all right. If Father O'Reilly had any criticism to make it was that none of the children had been brought up in the True Faith and to go to Mass and Confession. "But there," he admitted frankly, "if Patrick had chosen to serve the Church of Rome rather than the Church of England we should have been deprived of the delightful company of Charlotte and Emily and by implication that of Jane Eyre and Catherine Earnshaw."

He asked me then what my particular religious denomination was and I told him I had been brought up a Wesleyan Methodist, though I had to admit to not being a regular chapel-goer. "Oh dear . . ." he remarked, blandly. "I'm afraid Charlotte had very little time for your lot. She had even less time for ours."

I said it surprised me somewhat that the family had managed to achieve so much from such comparatively humble beginnings. "Burning the midnight oil," said Father O'Reilly, "or rather rushlight candles in Patrick's case. The Bible, Paradise Lost and Pilgrim's Progress . . . they were his main sources of study, plus a bit of head-puzzling over Greek and Latin primers. That way he got to be a teacher in the local primary school and later, with a certain amount of string-pulling, he was enabled to enter St. John's College, Cambridge, where he obtained his B.A. degree in Divinity. Certainly he got a much better start in life than his old man who had to rub along on the few shillings a week he earned as a farm-labourer. That tumbledown cottage you saw cost him no more than about a couple of bob a month in rent but it was just about as much as he could afford at the time."

We bowled into Newry just after that and I said goodbye, rather sadly, to my knowledgeable companion. "You've been drinking!" my aunt exclaimed when at last I presented myself for her inspection. It was on my breath, that's all, and no more than the lingering effects of a couple of wee drams of the real Irish ("Not a drop is sold

3

till it's seven years old."). I could hardly let Father O'Reilly depart without a final toast to that particular Immortal Memory.

☆   ☆ ☆   ☆

I was last in Emdale in 1974 and I didn't linger there long on account of the "troubles" and the chance of a stray bullet, bomb, or booby-trap. Patrick's birthplace had been tidied up considerably since I first saw it and a commemorative plaque attached by the Irish Tourist Board for the information of anyone brave or foolhardy enough to run the gauntlet between Belfast and Newry. A great pity really . . . Were all as peaceful in Haworth some of its annual 100,000 visitors might well have been tempted to stray further afield, to the benefit of old Ireland's national economy.

My maiden aunt has long since taken up residence in that happy land where all differences of opinion, whether religious or political, were settled once and for all with the fall of Lucifer. She never quite cottoned on to the Brontes but at least she was spared the sorrow and anguish the like good people of Belfast have been called upon to endure, to say nothing of those in her own home town.

☆   ☆ ☆   ☆

Chapter 2

ST. JOHN'S COLLEGE, CAMBRIDGE (1802 - 1806)

THOUGH I HAVE always supported the Dark as opposed to the Light Blues in the University Boat Race I have never ceased to prefer Cambridge to Oxford as a seat of learning.

Maybe it is because I consider Cambridge to be the least reactionary of the two establishments for there is, after all, a generation gap of some forty years between them. Oxford's first "University College" was recorded as such in 1249. Its Cambridge equivalent, "Peterhouse" was founded in 1284.

Cambridge, in fact, originated as an offshoot of Oxford. Some of the more militant among the latter university's students migrated there after a spot of bother with the local townspeople. Such disputes between Town and Gown were always a common feature of University life. The tradition persists in the glass and concrete educational establishments of our own times.

Notable among the dissentient voices raised in the quiet water-meadows along Cam-side were those of Thomas Cranmer of Jesus College and Hugh Latimer of Clare. Both were branded as religious heretics and both were burnt at the stake in, of all places, Oxford. Almost equally heretical were the theories later propounded by Charles Darwin of Christ's in his "Origin of Species" and the impact made on 20th Century physical science by Professors Thompson and Rutherford at the famous Cavendish Laboratory. Sir Isaac Newton himself studied mathematics and physics at Trinity in 1661. The tree outside the Great Gate there is reputed to be a descendant of the one from which fell an apple almost as epoch-making as that by which Adam was tempted in the Garden of Eden.

Three famous poets, all remarkable for their unorthodox opinions, are associated with Christ's College, Corpus Christi and Trinity: John Milton, as much for his pamphlet

5

on Divorce as for "Paradise Lost"; Kit Marlowe, for the political intrigues which ended in his cloak and dagger assassination in a Deptford tavern; and Lord Byron, arch-enemy of moral and religious humbug. To be sure, a more traditional balance was struck by Wordsworth at St. John's and Rupert Brooke (most popular and sentimentally orthodox of modern poets) at King's. Nearby Grantchester is still regarded as something of a literary shrine.

A comparatively insignificant versifier (one hesitates calling him poet) was a fellow-student for at least a year at St. John's with the notorious author of "Childe Harold" and "Don Juan". For altogether different reasons, however, his reputation can be said to have lasted as long and to have worn as well.

This was the Rev. Patrick Bronte, father of Charlotte and Anne, two of England's most famous woman novelists; father, too, of Emily, who as the creator of "Wuthering Heights" must be regarded as one of the greatest writers of all time.

☆   ☆ ☆   ☆

I cannot help thinking that 25-year old Patrick was already something of a snob when, in 1802, he first entered the imposing gateway of St. John's College with its decorative motif of daisies, or marguerites, particularising the arms of its foundress as those of Lady Margaret Beaufort, mother of the Tudor dynasty.

In spite, or perhaps because of, his humble Irish origin, he was a fervent supporter of the hierarchy and one not immune to the flattery of those in authority. This was borne out by his youthful hero-worshipping of Nelson and Wellington and his proud boast of having served alongside the young Lord Palmerston in the Volunteer Corps raised by the University to counter the threat of a Napoleonic invasion. In later life, too, he went out of his way to encourage his daughter Charlotte's friendship with Sir James Kay-Shuttleworth, in opposition to her own personal inclinations. At the same time he was all against her marrying his curate, Arthur Bell Nicholls, on account of his lowly position and prospects. There was, indeed, much of the snob in Mr Bronte's otherwise estimable character.

This particular trait first manifested itself when his name was inadvertently entered in the College registers as "Branty" instead of "Brunty", an opportunity seized on by Patrick to have it set down as "Bronte". The substitution, he thought, was sufficiently justified by the fact that Nelson had recently been created Duke of Bronte and the new boy at St. John's saw no reason why he should not share a little of the reflected glory. Later, to further emphasise the distinction, he adopted the diaerisis (i.e. the sign ¨) as an accentuation of the second vowel sound, much to the mortification and disgust of latterday printers.

Nevertheless, Patrick Bronte remained one of the poorest of poor students in spite of having entered St. John's as a "sizar" at reduced fees. In order to supplement his meagre financial resources he set about obtaining as many scholarships (or exhibitions) as possible. In the latter part of his residence too, before obtaining his B.A. degree in Divinity, he was allotted an annual grant from the Church Missionary Society's Fund.

One must respect the literal "nose to the grindstone" way in which he applied himself to his students and the furtherance of his career. One must admire too the fact that in spite of his frugal circumstances he somehow contrived to make a regular allowance to his mother in Ireland and continued to do so until her death in 1822. What he would have thought of the radical changes in the students and the buildings of Cambridge is problematical. One likes to think he would have approved in some ways for, traditional as he might have been, he was never a reactionary. When the Luddites broke up the newly-installed labour-saving machinery in the woollen mills of the West Riding his sympathies were almost equally divided between management and workers, between those who would maintain and those who rebelled against authority. Nevertheless, he always kept a revolver handy as a precaution against things getting out of control on one side or the other.

Mr Bronte would find a great deal unchanged in modern Cambridge for universities, as a general rule, are built to last and to resist change. That he would appreciate the Bridge of Sighs, erected over the River Cam some twenty-five years after he left to take up his first curacy at Wethersfield in Essex, I do not doubt. Everybody else does. Also he may well have considered Sir George Gilbert Scott's new Gothic Chapel at St. John's an improvement on the mediaeval one it replaced, more especially after hearing the college choir's annual Ascension Day concert from the top of its tower.

The Cam, of course, continues to meander gently for miles through fields, commons and cottage gardens, but the town of some 9,000 or so inhabitants he once knew has grown into a city with a population of well over 100,000, stretching out its tentacles to encompass the outlying villages of Cherry Hinton and Chesterton and completely swallowing neighbouring Girton. Nor, dedicated as he was to burning the midnight oil, can we expect Patrick to have taken much interest in the social occasion of May Week (held in June) with its expensive balls and the equally popular "Bumps" (when 15 boats, 1½ lengths behind each other, strain to achieve the traditional ceremony of colliding with the one in front). As a physically well set-up young Irishman, however, he may well have been inclined to try for his 'Blue' when the Cambridge men adjourned for their preliminary training at Ely. Unfortunately he would have been much too old for that annual scampering between Putney and Mortlake.

One wonders what he would have made of the fact that three colleges are now devoted solely to the education of the female sex, though Charlotte would undoubtedly have approved. And what about the institution of Family Planning at the Kingsway Clinic in Carlton Way and the Advisory Centre for Young People in Clarendon Street? Even Charlotte would have been shocked, though Emily might well have taken it in her stride. Certainly poor Mrs Bronte, whose short married life was occupied almost entirely with the business of child-bearing, could have done with something of that kind. With her it was a case of Hobson's Choice (so firmly associated with the Cambridge carrier whose custom it was to hire out his horses in strict rotation).

☆   ☆ ☆   ☆

In the otherwise excellent brochure put out as Tourist Information by the Publicity Department of the City of Cambridge there is no mention of Patrick Bronte's name among those who have graced that fair city in passing. Nor is there any reason why it should be, I suppose, for he achieved no lasting fame in his own right except as being one worthy parson among many of his kind. How different for Cambridge it might have been if Charlotte, Emily, and Anne could have attended college at Girton, Newnham, or New Hall. Or would their genius have flowered so well in that particular soil or been recognised as such among their modern counterparts?

☆   ☆ ☆   ☆

Chapter 3

WETHERSFIELD, ESSEX (1806 - 1809)

RECENTLY I TOOK the Eastern National bus down the B1053 from Braintree to Wethersfield, a distance of approximately seven miles, through the same green countryside Patrick Bronte once strolled in with his lady-love, Mary Burder.

In outward appearance the small Essex village would seem to have changed very little from the time when young Mr Bronte took up his first curacy there in the autumn of 1806. The house under whose roof he lodged with Miss Mildred Davy, spinster of this parish, still overlooks the clump of plane trees on the triangular village green though he would be at pains to appreciate the significance of the adjoining garage with its row of petrol pumps. The 13th Century tower of the church of St. Mary Magdalene still contrives to make the surrounding small villas, cottages and shops look vaguely impermanent. Its 20th Century pyramidal roof and copper spire, however, might well have struck him as passing strange and slightly ridiculous.

The old Dissenters' Chapel in which Mary Burder contrarily worshipped might be expected to revive unpleasant associations in connection with that ill-fated liaison. Otherwise he would have little difficulty in recognising it, apart from its having been superficially restored in 1822 and the fact that its dissenting congregation now gather together under the all-embracing umbrella of the United Reform denomination.

The present vicar of Patrick's old parish church referred in a recent issue of the parish magazine to local field names over the years having tended to disappear in favour of Ordnance Survey grid-references. Nostalgically he regretted the passing of such landmarks as "Bouncers", "Hither

Stubbs", "Little Truckets" and "Round Robins". He rather pointedly mentioned "The Bottom" too as being farmed by one rejoicing in the name of John Burder. This must undoubtedly have struck a responsive chord in the heart of the Rev. Patrick Bronte if one is prepared to adopt the assumption that he might be still wandering somewhere among what still remains of the neighbouring shades.

☆   ☆ ☆   ☆

Some time early in 1807 18-year old Mary Burder came like a ray of Spring sunshine into the rather faded, almost autumnal atmosphere of Patrick's lodgings at St. George's House. Miss Mildred Davy, it transpired, was not only the young curate's landlady; she was Mary's maiden aunt.

The couple were immediately attracted to one another, as well they might be under the circumstances, though whether the fact should be attributed to Patrick's good fortune or his bad luck depends entirely upon which way you incline to look at it.

The fly in the ointment was undoubtedly the aforementioned John Burder's only brother, a man of some substance living at that time over at Yeldham, a village some five or six miles north-east of Wethersfield. John having died at the early age of 40, just prior to Patrick's arrival in the neighbourhood, his widow and four surviving children (of whom Mary was the oldest) were of necessity taken into this man's protective care and control.

His obligations in that respect he interpreted as extending to his young niece and the overseeing of her prospects in the matrimonial field. Hearing how matters stood between her and Patrick (they were as good as engaged at the time) he made it his business to enquire most diligently into her would-be husband's credentials, his antecedents, and his immediate expectations. What he found (or did not find) there confirmed his already formed opinion that such a union was on no account to be entertained.

As a self-made man he had no time for indigent parsons, more especially one who was obviously of 'bog-Irish' extraction and not prepared to come clean with regard to

11

his background and family connections. He might well have a B.A. degree and influential friends at Cambridge, as he never tired of boasting, but that was no guarantee that he would ever be capable of keeping Mary in the style to which she was accustomed. Moreover, it had come to his ears that the young fool indulged in the reprehensible habit of writing Poetry. He would sooner have entertained a drunkard or a clown than a time-waster of that kind.

The upshot was that Mary was moved to his more immediate protective custody at Yeldham and out of Patrick's sphere of influence for good and all. Though he wrote her a long and pleading letter she did not deign to answer it and he could only conclude that she was content to abide by the decision that had been made for her. It was enough. The disillusioned young curate immediately made preparations for extending his ministrations elsewhere and on the 7th January 1809 he left Wethersfield well and truly behind him and set his face resolutely towards Wellington in Shropshire where a new appointment had been arranged for him.

☆   ☆ ☆   ☆

In view of the lasting fame he was later to attain through the medium of his marriage to Maria Branwell of Penzance and the God-sent gift of their three daughters, Charlotte, Emily, and Anne, one would have thought that Patrick Bronte was well done with Mary Burder and Wethersfield for the rest of his natural life. Skeletons are best kept behind closed doors, securely barred and padlocked too.

Mr Bronte's life, however, was anything but a natural one. Mary was snatched from him almost literally from the altar steps. He relinquished Maria to the Angel of Death and the cold flagstones of Haworth parish church. Of the six children left in his sole care, little Maria (aged 11) and Elizabeth (aged 10) died within five weeks of each other and Branwell (his only son), Emily and Anne within a period of only eight months. Charlotte had not reached her 39th birthday when she followed them to the grave, the same age in fact as her ill-fated mother.

Who, in those circumstances, could possibly accuse Mr Bronte of being inconsistent in character? Admitted that when he contacted his former sweetheart again he had yet to bear the full brunt of all that tragedy, but contact her he did. It was excusable in a man recently bereaved and with half a dozen young children on his hands that he should, after a decent interval, set about securing a replacement for the mother they lacked. Who better than one with whom he had not only had personal relations but those of a most intimate kind?

He unburdened himself to Mary in no uncertain fashion. His letter, though well written, was incredibly naive, almost pathetic. He had thought for some years, he said, that it was highly probable she was married, but from enquiries previously made he was glad she was still single and selfish enough to wish she might remain so. In one breath he refers to the sickness and death of his dear wife and in the next to the fact that his ancient love has been rekindled and that he has a longing desire to see her again. The obvious disadvantage of having six young children to support is skipped over by euphemistically dismissing them as "a small but sweet little family" and, of course, he again feels called upon to boast of having influential friends and connections. He even refers her to one of them for a character reference! The letter, in short, is a triumph both of over-statement and under-statement.

Mary Burder's reply is one of the best examples in all literature of controlled vituperation. In reviewing her former situation in the light of her present circumstances she cannot help feeling "increased gratitude and thankfulness to that wise, that indulgent providence which then watched over me for good and withheld me from forming in very early life an indissoluble engagement with one whom I cannot think was altogether clear of duplicity." She is glad that she has in no way hindered his promotion or caused any of "those great and affluent friends" he used to write and speak of from withholding their patronage on her account, "young, inexperienced, unsuspecting, and ignorant" as she then was. From having herself lost a brother, since they last met, she can "truly sympathise with you and the poor little innocents in your bereavement". She cannot resist, however, the ultimate sting in the tail: "The Lord can supply all your and their need," she says. "It gives me pleasure always to hear the work of the Lord prospering." It is game, set, and match so far as Mary is concerned.

Poor Patrick . . . Life is full of 'ifs' and 'buts' – but one thing is certain. If the course of true love had run smoothly for him and Mary in Wethersfield its consummation could not possibly have bequeathed to us so remarkable a literary heritage as that contained in "Jane Eyre" and "Wuthering Heights". Again, if Mary had later consented to mother the Rev. Patrick Bronte's "small but sweet little family" might she not ultimately have smothered with loving kindness the seed that by its very nature could only flourish and flower in stony ground? It is a sombre and sobering thought.

☆   ☆ ☆   ☆

Chapter 4

WELLINGTON, SHROPSHIRE (1809)

MR BRONTE CAME to Wellington in January 1809 as curate of All Saints' Church. It was a matter of necessity as much as choice. He wanted as speedily as possible to forget Wethersfield in Essex and his ill-fated love affair with Mary Burder. He was in the position of one seeking a convalescent home after a period of almost mortal sickness.

His choice of Wellington was influenced by an old friend of his university days, the Rev. John Nunn, at that time a curate at St. Chad's Church in Shrewsbury. I have particular reason to remember that church myself, having been married there in the dark winter of 1940. It is completely circular in design, a fact of which I am continually reminded whenever I approach the Albert Hall across Kensington Gardens.

The very name "Wellington" must have sounded much like a trumpet call in Mr Bronte's ears. The Iron Duke, Arthur Wellesley, was a man he particularly admired and his children, especially Charlotte, were later brought up almost to hero-worship him. Indeed, it has been said of the Rev. Patrick Bronte that had not circumstances conspired to make him a parson he might equally have served his country with musket and pike.

Not for nothing was his daughter Emily affectionately referred to as "The Major". There was a great deal of the same quality in both her physical and mental make-up.

☆   ☆ ☆   ☆

The Wellington of the early 19th Century was very different from that which has now virtually been taken over by Telford New Town. By comparison with the small, though prosperous, farming community of Wethersfield it

15

was a rather poverty-stricken place in spite of being already highly industrialised. As the present day publicity brochure is at pains to recall "Dramatic developments (were) taking place in the nearby coalfield, where a 'world's first' was achieved in many important fields of iron technology, coke-smelting, etc." One of the largest steam engines in England consumed "upwards of twenty tons of coal every twenty-four hours." Wellington was certainly thriving in some directions but the consequent prospect opened in others was anything but rosy.

Fortunes were undoubtedly being made by the mine-owners but the miners can scarcely be said to have had their fair share of it. In common with the great majority of the working people of that time they existed at near starvation level with the option of unemployment, the workhouse, or service in the French Wars if they did not choose to man the daily treadmill.

These people, predominantly working-class, made up by far the greater part of the flock entrusted to Patrick Bronte's personal charge.

☆   ☆ ☆   ☆

Not altogether unlike his latterday counterpart, Vincent van Gogh, who in Isleworth, Ramsgate, and his native Borinage opted to preach the gospel to the poor and needy before taking up pencil and brush, Mr Bronte put his whole heart and soul into relieving conditions as he found them among the pit-workers of Wellington. He visited and held prayer meetings in their miserable cottage homes, was often to be seen at the pithead itself, and on more than one occasion is reported to have assisted in rescue operations at the coalface. In that way he undoubtedly won the respect if not the affection of a dour mining community which in general had little of either to spare for those whose business it was to extend the Kingdom of God among the "dark, satanic mills" of England's green and pleasant land.

It must be remembered, of course, that Patrick was comparatively young and active at that time (in his 32nd year, to be exact) and as tough and virile as one might expect of the first-born son of Irish peasant stock. Only grief wore him out as the years went by, constant grief at the continuing loss of those he held most dear. At 85, with no-one left but Arthur Bell Nicholls, the son-in-law he had once despised, he was more than willing to call a halt in the service of the Lord who had so chastised him.

He spent little less than a year in Wellington (from early January to early December) before taking up his first Yorkshire appointment as curate to the Rev. John Buckworth, vicar of the parish church of Dewsbury in the West Riding. Yorkshire was ultimately to boast of being the birthplace and workshop of his three immortal daughters, Charlotte, Emily and Anne, but Shropshire has almost as much cause to be proud of the part it played in making that initial move possible. Essex abandoned him no less than he abandoned Essex, for he seems always to have been treated as something of a stranger there. Indeed, had it not been for the very real friends he met in Wellington, men like John Fennell and William Morgan, it is doubtful whether he would ever have been recommended for the promotion he deserved. Certainly he would not have been in the right place at the right time to have met and married John Fennell's niece, Maria Branwell from Penzance.

It was William Morgan who performed that ceremony before taking turn and turn about in himself being married to Maria's cousin Jane. Morgan it was, too, who later christened Mr Bronte's three famous daughters and officiated at the funeral of his wife, mercifully released from the agony of internal cancer.

John Nunn of St. Chad's, instrumental in obtaining Patrick's Wellington appointment, later married a girl from Shrewsbury. It may well have been Mr Bronte's fate to marry a local girl from Wethersfield and it is doubtful then if we should have been blessed with the authors of Jane Eyre, Wuthering Heights, and The Tenant of Wildfell Hall, more especially if one takes into account the wild moorland scenery against the background of which such masterpieces were composed.

17

Commercially viable (dreadful phrase) as Wellington was even in Mr Bronte's time, it had some compensation for the nature lover in the 600 million year old Wrekin (all 1,300 feet of it). Whatever Telford New Town contrives to foist on its contracted partner in the way of so-called redevelopment and improvement it can do nothing about levelling off the Wrekin for an extended car park, office block, or shopping complex.

Apart from being continually reminded of his native County Down and in particular its never to be forgotten Mountains of Mourne Mr Bronte would find much still unchanged in what remains one of the most delightful areas of country scenery in the four kingdoms. As one who loved walking in company with a dog and a shillelagh he must often have tramped the ten or so miles there and back to the picturesque village of Little Wenlock and even further afield to Much Wenlock itself with its 7th Century abbey (albeit in ruins) and its charming Elizabethan Manor House, Shipton Hall, with its stone-walled gardens. One can only regret that as a poet himself (if by no means a very good one) he was denied the melancholy pleasure of reading A.E. Housman there . . . "'Tis time, I think, by Wenlock town/The golden broom should blow . . ." So far as Time was concerned the author of "A Shropshire Lad" was little more than a babe in arms when Patrick died at Haworth in 1861.

The old man would still have been young enough, however, to have read with interest the news of the opening up of the through-road to Holyhead in 1835, designed to allow the Irish members of parliament quick access to Westminster. Admitted, they still had to travel by coach but now the journey would be completed in one day! "The Wonder", for instance, left Shrewsbury every morning at 4.45 and arrived in London by 10 p.m. Passengers from Wellington were picked up around 6 a.m. at the old Falcon Inn in Haygate Road.

In that respect the recently designated Telford New Town would not strike Mr Bronte as altogether strange. It was Thomas Telford, one of his contemporaries and for some years Surveyor-General of Shropshire who, as a civil engineer and road and bridge-builder, made the miracle of "The Wonder" possible. That he was also an intimate friend of the poet Southey would have endeared him to the Bronte family even more.

☆   ☆ ☆   ☆

Chapter 5

DEWSBURY, YORKSHIRE (1809 - 1811)

THREE BUILDINGS struck me in particular when I first visited Dewsbury: the ancient (though much restored) parish church; the 19th Century Town Hall — and the 20th Century rectangular glass and concrete structure housing the offices of the Ministry of Health and Social Security. All were comparatively close together.

Once the proud centre of the West Riding woollen industry Dewsbury is still dwarfed by several huge (and seemingly smokeless) chimneys. They appear to sprout straight from the ground like hollow tree-trunks without branch or foliage. Over all are the impressive Pennine heights of Westboro' and Crackenedge, crowned with stone dwelling houses to and from which it would seem impossible to proceed on business and home again without the aid of a moving staircase.

At the bottom of the bowl, so to speak, winds the gentle, shy, almost unobtrusive little river Calder.

☆   ☆ ☆   ☆

Dewsbury is proud of having featured in William the Conqueror's Domesday (or Doomsday) Book of 1086. Tradition has it that Paulinus, the Roman missionary, preached on the site of the present parish church as long ago as AD 627.

Be that as it may, what is not disputed is the fact that the Rev. Patrick Bronte first set foot here in Yorkshire on being appointed curate in December 1809 to the then vicar, John Buckworth, himself a fine preacher and popular writer of hymns. Yorkshire, and in particular the West Riding, has been justifiably proud of the Brontes from that day to this.

I recall attending morning service in Patrick's old church and sitting almost directly under the brass wall-plaque recording all his ministerial appointments from 1806, when he left St. John's College, Cambridge, to his death at Haworth in 1861. In a neighbouring pew a young mother studiously ignored the fact that her small son was completely absorbed in a copy of either "Beano" or "The Dandy". It was obviously one way of keeping him quiet during what, for him, must have seemed a long and boring sermon.

I could have sworn I saw Mr Bronte's head (in profile) half-turned in his direction and it was more than my imagination that he seemed to be registering the strongest disapproval . . .

As a matter of fact Mr Bronte was never all that fond of children, even when on their best behaviour. There was some excuse for him, of course, in having been left with six little ones on his hands when his wife died within 18 months of the family's arrival in Haworth. Maybe it was a good thing in some ways that he inclined to leave them too much to their own devices. It enabled his famous daughters, Charlotte, Emily, and Anne to develop their literary talents ("like potatoes growing in a cellar") without let or hindrance from either restrictive or over-indulgent parents. That his only son, poor Branwell, should have run to seed in consequence was no part of his bargain with the Almighty.

In spite of his obsession with solitariness, however, the good people of Dewsbury had cause to bless his protective care of their own children. There was that time, for instance, when he was instrumental in saving a local street arab from death by drowning in the icy waters of the Calder; that other occasion, too, when he stood up bravely to a drunken lout who attempted to bar the progress of a party of Sunday School children on their 'Whitsun Walk' to and from the neighbouring village of Earlsheaton. If not exactly loved, Patrick was looked up to with a great deal of respect by the poor among his parishioners.

They were troublesome times for the people of the West Riding. Already murmurs of discontent were beginning to be heard among the handloom weavers and the mill-operatives in their scattered stone cottages on account of the threatened installation of labour-saving machinery. This was to erupt finally in the notorious Luddite Riots and the armed attack on Rawfolds Mill out at Liversedge, between Heckmondwike and Cleckheaton, so graphically portrayed by Charlotte Bronte in her novel "Shirley".

Meanwhile, however, Patrick was always on hand to give consolation and advice where it was most sorely needed. He was constantly to be met with striding across country with some neighbour's dog at his heels and clutching a precautionary shillelagh, as befitting a true-born Ulsterman. Though generally dressed in the familiar black suit and white cravat of later photographs, he was at that time a tall, handsome, auburn-haired young man of 34. One can imagine how often a more than admiring glance was cast in his direction by the unattached females of the neighbouring hills and valleys.

☆   ☆ ☆   ☆

Mr Bronte would undoubtedly find much changed in the Dewsbury he once knew but he would find a good deal pretty much the same as it was then. The 13th Century Moot Hall, for instance, and those fortress-like walls encircling the town at broken intervals, which give one the impression of having strayed into some medieval pocket-size city with Northgate and Westgate crying out, surely, for some lost portcullis and grilled doorway. The almost continuous flow of cars and lorries and the unbroken rows of modern multiple stores would probably send him packing for good, though God knows where . . . As for that fantastically old-fashioned Victorian Town Hall from whose grotesque bell-tower the quarter-chimes ring out all day and night, culminating in a booming though slightly hesitant insistence that the hour is later than you think . . . I don't think he would have reacted at all well to that.

"It's got a bit of a cold in the throat from standing out there all that time in the rain," was one local resident's delivered opinion. It failed to console me for the fact that my hotel bedroom was almost cheek by jowl with it.

That particular clock, I found, had a twin brother (or sister) some short distance away, ornamenting (of all things) the local Co-operative stores. It chimed always, or at least whilst I was there, a few seconds behind its soul-mate, as though struggling desperately to keep up with the running. I liked it the better of the two, however, if only for its comparatively modest performance, though I might have felt differently on slightly closer acquaintance.

What Patrick and his daughters would have thought of the Ministry of Health and Social Security and its steady stream of customers I cannot possibly imagine. Somehow I don't think they would altogether have approved.

On the other hand I incline to think they would have regarded not unfavourably the immigrant population of Indians and Pakistanis, so much a feature of this and other West Riding towns which have utilised their traditional skills to supplement the local work-force. That Sunday morning, after church, I came on a rather disconsolate little group of them squatting on their doorsteps in a sadly faded part of town much as countless other immigrants once did (and still do now) in the back streets of Whitechapel. It intrigued me to see lines of gaily-coloured washing strung out from window to window across their small cul-de-sac and at first I thought it was some peculiar native custom that had penetrated into our modern world. Later I was to observe the same thing in evidence at the foot of Main Street in Haworth, but this time practised by the direct descendants of Patrick's former parishioners there. It would seem that no stranger to our shores is long in following the beaten tracks or adhering strictly to established guide-lines. Integration with a vengeance, surely?

At least in Dewsbury the coloured population have already set up their own HABIB Bank, albeit occupying the most unassuming of corner-shop premises. Given time it may well compete with the more opulent of its Western counterparts. These people are nothing if not industrious, thrifty, and hard-working and a great many of us can well profit by their example.

I have heard tell that every workaday night in Dewsbury the "10 o'clock Gun" is loosed off from some local mill-yard to let the owners know that all is well Luddite-wise. I never heard it myself but the sound may conceivably have been drowned by those twin clocks. Also I was given to understand that every Christmas Eve the "Devil's Knell" is tolled from the church tower, once for every year since Christ was born, but I was not prepared to wait another six months on that eventuality.

Before leaving for home I took a turn round the beautifully extended churchyard with its park-like green lawns and its rest-benches for the old folk in the summer-evening shades. Patrick, I'm sure, would have liked to linger there with me though, like me, he would have sought in vain some trace of his former vicarage lodgings among the dust and ashes of the far from immortal dead.

He could, of course, have got a bus from the station just round the corner which would have taken him out to Liversedge in next to no time at all. From there another bus would have conveyed him just as swiftly up to his old vicarage at Hightown. He would only have to ask the conductor for the stop at Clough Lane, Hartshead. Everybody knows it round there and most people know what it stands for. As with the brass tablet in Dewsbury Church it is plainly marked for all who care to see.

☆   ☆ ☆   ☆

Chapter 6

HARTSHEAD, YORKSHIRE (1811 - 1815)

THE TOWN CENTRE in Heckmondwike was ablaze with red geraniums and bursting at the seams with Saturday morning shoppers when I first got off the bus there. It is a crying shame that some London dramatic critics refer to this place disparagingly as providing coach-loads of trippers for the more popular Wednesday afternoon matinees. If it's fun these people want then Batley's famous Night Club is a much better bet and cheap at half the price.

Next-door Liversedge is dull, almost shabby-looking, by comparison with Heckmondwike. But Liversedge has had all the notoriety it needs, and a bit more. Charlotte Bronte put it on the map for good in describing the attack on Rawfolds Mill there in Chapter XIX of her novel "Shirley".

"A crash — smash — shiver — stopped their whispers. A simultaneously hurled volley of stones had saluted the broad front of the mill, with all its windows; and now every pane of every lattice lay in shattered and pounded fragments. A yell followed this demonstration — a rioters' yell — a North of England — a Yorkshire — a West Riding — a West Riding — clothing-district of Yorkshire rioters' yell . . ."

Charlotte's father had himself been involved in the real-life attack on Rawfolds Mill. When he moved from Dewsbury in March 1811 to take up his new appointment as "perpetual curate" at St. Peter's Church in neighbouring Hartshead, troops of red-coated cavalry were already beginning to patrol the lonely stretches of moorland country as a precaution against the threat of trouble from disgruntled workers in the woollen industry. The intro-duction of new labour-saving machinery in Nottingham, Leicester and Derbyshire had led to mass unemployment and the consequent reduction of the weavers' standard of

25

living to a near starvation level. This threat was now menacing the operatives of the West Riding area and they were in the process of taking militant action to defend their livelihoods.

The same men who but a short time previously had paraded and drilled in Home Guard fashion against the threat of Napoleonic invasion now took to drilling at dead of night as a preliminary to what the authorities feared might well end in another Peasants' Revolt, even full-scale Civil War. Stirred up by those who had already suffered from what they considered to be the mill-owners' high-handed action and (as is usual in such cases) by paid agitators from outside the industry and the locality, they were at first content with attacking and destroying the machinery brought in by individual waggon-loads. On the night of Sunday, the 12th of April, 1812, however, they rose to the attack in much more deadly earnest.

Rawfolds Mill at Liversedge, some two miles from Patrick Bronte's parish of Hartshead-cum-Clifton, was their agreed target. About 100 men armed with muskets and hatchets and almost anything else they could lay their hands on made a frontal attack on the mill just after midnight when they fondly imagined they had the best chance of overwhelming any possible opposition. Unfortunately, they reckoned without William Cartwright, the owner, who having been previously tipped off as to what was afoot had taken the necessary steps to protect his property. With the aid only of some half-dozen soldiers and a slightly less number of 'loyal' workmen (who would today have been regarded as 'black-legs') he succeeded in beating off the attack and sending the attackers flying in complete disorder.

Wherever one's sympathies might lie in this affair the fact remains that the workers, in all ways, got by far the worst of it. Many were wounded in that night's affray; some died. Cartwright, aided and abetted by the Rev. Hammond Roberson (a militant parson, if ever there was one) tracked down both the ring-leaders and the most faint-hearted of their supporters. Some were executed, others transported for life. So harsh, indeed, were the penal laws of the time exacted that the Leeds Mercury actually reported one of the mill's *defenders* as being sentenced to 300 lashes for refusing to fire on his own brothers whom he recognised as taking part in the assault. Cartwright himself couldn't stomach that much and on his own recommendation the sentence was finally reduced to 25 lashes only.

Patrick Bronte's part in this affair was a peculiar one. As a comparatively newly-arrived minister in the locality and, by implication, a supporter of the Establishment, he was, of necessity, compelled to respect the rule of law and order. On the other hand, as one who had himself been subject to poverty and privation during his childhood and early youth he had a great deal of sympathy with the workers and the cause they represented even if he did not altogether agree with the action they took to remedy their situation. In the circumstances he undoubtedly helped, insofar as he was able, to undo some of the harm that was done, tending those among the wounded who were brought to his attention and turning the proverbial blind eye to those he suspected of being escapees from summary justice. The attitude he adopted, in fact, was not unlike that of the Quakers in wartime who feel it their christian duty to treat with friend and foe on equal terms.

Nevertheless, it was round about this time that he first purchased a pistol for his own personal protection. He continued to keep it in sound working order for so long as he still had the strength and courage to make use of it.

☆ ☆ ☆ ☆

'The road runs up hill all the way' to St. Peter's Church at Hartshead, overlooking the almost breath-taking view of the Calder Valley. I did not wait for the bus but set off walking rather vaguely in the direction of Hightown and the three-storey stone house at the top of Clough Lane which Patrick Bronte was to rent later on in his marriage to Maria Branwell of Penzance and where his first two children, Maria and Elizabeth, were born.

I went off the track on a couple of occasions. First I

found myself in the burial ground of Christ Church at Liversedge and only recollected that this was in fact the church which Hammond Roberson (the militant parson) built for himself on leaving St. Peter's, when I stumbled on his grave there. Nearby (some would say as fitting company) was the grave of William Cartwright, the owner of Rawfolds Mill.

On the second occasion, having feasted my eyes on Patrick's stone vicarage facing directly up Clough Lane, I set myself to walk the so-called "mile" down through a deep hollow and up again to St. Peter's which he regularly trod to work and back home again. The church I eventually stumbled on was almost too grotesque to be true till I realised I was wandering among the tombstones of Liversedge Cemetery (circa 1903!).

From thence I must have walked at least another mile out of my way. On a hill-top edge I came suddenly on a cluster of new houses beside a straggling high-road. Two young girls in jeans and jumpers were busy weeding one of the back gardens.

"St. Peter's Church?" I enquired. "Any idea where it is?"

They conferred together in agitated whispers and it was obvious they were anything but certain themselves, though prepared to argue about it. One of them eventually approached the fence over which I was leaning. "If you look straight through there," she said, pointing up an alley between their house and the next, "you'll see a church tower away in the distance. We think it might be that."

She seemed sympathetically aware that I hadn't got a car.

☆   ☆ ☆   ☆

It was ages before I homed, pigeon-like, on what kept on eluding me between roof-tops and trees. It was a squat little yellow church, not unlike a decaying back tooth, poised literally on the edge of nowhere. "Greatly restored in 1881 — the old tower still survives — also some Norman arches in the south porch and chancel" was the description

I had of it in my notebook. Obviously St. Peter's, though there was nothing to indicate the fact. Also it was locked fast; if against present-day vandals, I was at a loss to know from whence they might be expected to attack.

The silence up there was so intense that even an occasional chirping sparrow was quite startling in effect. Far down in the widespread Calder Valley some tall chimneys were lazily smoking in the sunshine. It was like being half-way up Everest.

I recollected that Patrick Bronte had found his ministry here simple by comparison with what he had been called upon to undertake in Dewsbury. His congregation was certainly much smaller, being well out of town, and his annual stipend of £62 (plus rent allowance) quite definitely reflected his jog-trotting circumstances. Nevertheless, it is safe to say that he enjoyed here what was probably the happiest period in the whole of his troubled life.

When he first arrived, on the 3rd of March 1811, he was a care-free batchelor content not to fuss over the fact that no vicarage was available and he would have to find lodgings in a neighbouring farm-house (known locally as "Lousey Thorn", for no specified reason). When he left the district in May 1815 to take up a new appointment at Thornton, near Bradford, it was in company with a wife and two young children and in contemplation of continued domestic bliss. For him the barometer was still set fair and he was not weather-prophet enough yet to be aware of the approaching storm.

☆   ☆ ☆   ☆

In January 1812 an Academy was opened at Woodhouse Grove, Apperley Bridge, near Bradford, for the purpose of educating the sons of Wesleyan ministers. It is still thriving at the present day.

The school's first headmaster was John Fennell with whom Mr Bronte had made acquaintance in Wellington. When casting around for someone competent enough to examine his pupils at the end of their summer term Mr Fennell's choice quite naturally alighted on Patrick. He was duly appointed visiting inspector at a nominal fee of around £12.

By a peculiar turn of circumstances William Morgan, Mr Bronte's other close Wellington friend, became engaged at that time to John Fennell's daughter Jane and was in firm expectation of marrying her before the year's end. With that prospect in view Jane's cousin, Maria Branwell, came on a protracted visit from Penzance in June 1812, ostensibly to assist with the wedding arrangements. At Woodhouse Grove she met Patrick Bronte on one of his infrequent appearances there.

Patrick was much taken with this neat little woman who, though quiet and unassuming and fervently religious, undoubtedly had a mind of her own which accorded well with his own way of thinking. One might describe her as a combination of forceful Charlotte and shy and retiring Anne. As a consequence of this attachment the young curate's "duty" visits to Woodhouse Grove became more and more frequent and the couple were soon regularly corresponding and walking out together.

On a summer afternoon visit to the nearby romantic ruins of Kirkstall Abbey, Patrick proposed they should follow the example of Maria's cousin Jane and his old friend William Morgan. To that end a double wedding was arranged to take place at Guiseley on the 29th of December 1812.

This time there was no objection from blustering, socially-conscious farming folk like 'Uncle' Burder of Wethersfield. The Branwells of Penzance were more than his equal on those grounds. Thomas Branwell, Maria's father, had been a prosperous merchant and local councillor and the whole family, as strong Methodists, were greatly respected in the town. Maybe the fact that Maria was more or less in the position of doing what she liked, having lost both her parents some three years previously, had much to do with influencing the rest of the family to agree readily with the arrangement. Indeed it was even proposed that Maria's own sister, Charlotte, should marry her cousin Joseph in the far-off parish church of Penzance on that same December day. Not merely a *double*, but a *treble* wedding, was surely something quite unique in any family.

"I think if our lives are spared twenty years hence I shall then pray for you with the same, if not greater, fervour and delight that I do now . . ." wrote tragic Maria to her tragic Patrick just prior to this happy occasion. I mused long and sadly on those words as I returned that day the way I had come.

☆   ☆ ☆   ☆

Chapter 7

INTERLUDE – GUISELEY, YORKSHIRE
(29 December 1812)

THEY'RE 'GRET' ones for fish and chips in Yorkshire. On the bus between Leeds and Otley, where I hoped to pick up the connection for Harrogate, I was advised to 'get aht now an' cross t'rooard for the best meal in the West Riding'. "There's nobbut tea and bun-shops in 'Arrogate" said my informant, a well-upholstered local housewife lumbered with the weekend's shopping bags.

It was lunchtime, anyway, and I felt hungry enough to take the hint. Nor was I ever to regret sampling the local delicacy. Indeed, I discovered later that the establishment in question had a reputation that extended far beyond county boundaries.

I knew I could pick up the bus to Otley anytime now and even one straight through to Harrogate if I waited a little longer. Being in no particular hurry I decided to linger awhile in the neighbourhood. What did they call this place? I enquired and someone informed me very pointedly that it was "Guiseley".

The name rang a bell somewhere but my memory failed to connect immediately. I wandered around somewhat aimlessly for a while and it was quite by accident that I came upon the parish church of St. Oswald.

"Here lies an honest man" said an old gravestone in the beautiful green churchyard. The doorway was certainly Norman and I judged the west tower to be 15th century. The interior was obviously more modern and appeared to have been restored on several occasions. I was particularly struck with the bobbin-ended pews.

A vacuum-cleaner was whirring away down one of the side aisles and its manipulator, a middle-aged man in cardigan and shirt-sleeves, bade me a gruff 'good afternoon'. "It's over there in t'corner," he said, and when I raised my eyebrows, "It's Bronte rails you wanted, worn't it?"

Of course I did, though I wasn't there with that particular purpose in mind and might well have remained unaware of it. "At this rail on Tuesday 29th December 1812," said the wall tablet in the old chancel, "Patrick Bronte Minister of Hartshead was married to Maria Branwell."

Underneath, in case of any remaining doubt, was added the following explanatory inscription: "Among the most famous writers of our country are numbered their three daughters Charlotte, Emily and Ann."

Later the sexton strolled in. I said I was staying for a few days up at Haworth and I couldn't help feeling that he inclined to look down his nose at the volunteered information. If not actually contemptuous of "the folk who lived on the hill" he was at least middling different. After all, I reflected, Mrs Gaskell had not deigned to mention Guiseley in her famous biography of the author of Jane Eyre. It was all Haworth, Haworth — nothing but Haworth. To add insult to injury the sexton informed me that some ignorant people, mostly southerners, had been overheard in Bradford and Leeds enquiring for "Gweesley" — of all places. As a Londoner I blushed, but said nowt.

☆   ☆ ☆   ☆

Had I been a visiting American rather than so obviously a Cockney I'm quite sure the first thing he would have pointed out to me would have been the memorial tablet to the Longfellow family. As it was, both men were at pains to inform me that the forbears of the Author of Hiawatha and The Village Blacksmith had for generations been born, married, and died in that parish. Indeed, in the industrial complex that Guiseley had long since become there were still families living in the immediate neighbourhood who bore that illustrious name.

Would I like to see the Registers? I was delighted, of course, and from a battered old cupboard in the Vestry the sexton lovingly produced the volume for the year 1812 at my particular request. The very last entry, in fact, recorded the unique double wedding of Miss Branwell and her cousin Jane Fennell, both from far-off Penzance. The respective bridegrooms, as ministers of the Church of England, took it in turn to perform the marriage ceremony for each other and the brides did duty for one another as bridesmaids.

There were no further entries for the year 1812, the remaining blank pages being ruled across. As the sexton knowledgeably informed me the Ross Act of that year superseded the old form of register in use until that time.

I would have left then, I suppose, had I not been detained to look at what both the sexton and his helpmate obviously considered to be their greatest communal treasure. It was the register containing the church's first recorded entries of births, marriages, and deaths, all jumbled up together and dating back to the latter part of the 16th century. One page had half-crumbled away and it seemed the others would disintegrate at the slightest touch, but the spider-like writing was still perfectly legible.

The eyes of both men glowed with justifiable pride. I felt that by comparison with those early records of the parish of Guiseley that which commemorated the wedding of Patrick Bronte and Maria Branwell was very small beer indeed.

☆ ☆ ☆ ☆

Chapter 8

HARTSHEAD (Continued)

I RETURNED TO Hartshead quite recently and even then couldn't muster up enough courage to knock at the door of Clough House and ask to be given a brief glimpse of the interior. One doesn't do this sort of thing of course, as everybody knows who has hesitated before the doors of houses they have once lived in and long been removed from. In this case also the place was obviously well lived in by strangers and anything but a museum devoted to relics of the past. I lingered a while, then continued reluctantly on my way. There was not the satisfaction to be had here that one has come to expect from the Parsonage House at Haworth.

On the bus back to Heckmondwike I got into conversation with a charming lady who echoed much the same sentiments that were in my mind. She was obviously a Bronte enthusiast or she would never have remarked on the fact that she had seen me gaping at the windows of Patrick and Maria's old lodgings in much the same way as hungry Victorian children once congregated outside the bakers' shops in East End slums.

"We take it for granted round here," said my informant, "Leastways those of us who happen to be aware that it is still standing and what it continues to stand for. The rest don't matter very much, do they? About as much as it matters to them, I should say."

I couldn't help thinking her attitude was rather a snobbish one and that of the intellectual snob than whom there is none worse. Nevertheless there was a great deal in what she said. It applies to everything we are interested in as opposed to everything we are not. One can prefer football to ballet and bingo to ballroom dancing. It's a matter of free choice after all but should never be allowed to become one of blind prejudice.

☆   ☆ ☆   ☆

In remarking on the fact that Clough House looked "well lived in" I should add that this was never more the case than when Patrick Bronte set up home there after his marriage to Maria Branwell. It may well be said that for the first time in his life the wandering Irish curate had something like a regular stake in the community. Till then he would seem to have drifted rather aimlessly from place to place and appointment to appointment as circumstances and opportunity presented themselves.

Nothing settles a man more than a marriage of convenience and from Mr Bronte's point of view that much at least was certain about the rather unlikely alliance he had made. Whether Mrs Bronte felt herself to be settled as comfortably is matter for conjecture though devoutly to be wished. In the first place (and perhaps on account of his peasant origin) he was undoubtedly an egoist par excellence. The quality he most lacked was that of being open-hearted and affectionate towards those most dependent upon him though he was never one to shirk his "duties" in that direction. But when sober issues were to be faced he elected to face them in much the same way as the Americans incline at heart to the policy of "splendid isolation". To lock himself up in his study, well away from all human contacts, whilst composing his quite striking sermons and awfully dull poems, became more and more his accepted way of life. Later, it was to get away from the prattle of his own children as much as anything else that he chose to absent himself from their company; a trait that was to be developed even more markedly in his daughters Charlotte and Emily and one reason why they failed so utterly in the handling of other people's children when entrusted to them as pupils.

Mrs Bronte, on the other hand, was comparatively soft and pliable though possessed of a great fund of common-sense and a simple, almost childlike faith in her Creator which stemmed from her strict Non-conformist upbringing.

She came from a comfortable middle class home in the warmest corner of the country and her reaction to the harsh Northern climate and wild surroundings of the West Riding in which it was now her fate to be settled could only have been one of patient and dogged endurance. Nor could it have been easy living with a man as self-centred as Patrick, though she was later to put on record the fact that he was always "good" to her which can be interpreted whichever way you choose. Of the half-dozen children she was to bring into that world before leaving them so tragically to more or less fend for themselves it was patient, gentle, nose-to-the-grindstone Anne who was most certainly like her.

What went a long way towards settling the marked difference between this oddly-assorted pair of lovers was the fact that neither of them could be referred to exactly as "spring chickens". Patrick was nearly 36 years old when he led her to the altar: Maria was not far short of 30. If either had had any wild oats still to be sown (and that could possibly have been applied only to Patrick) the time would appear to have long since gone when they felt any inclination to scatter them. To this must be added the fact that both were equally dedicated to the service of God's work on earth and in heaven and were not to be dissuaded from it by any outside influence whatsoever.

From a purely materialistic point of view too Patrick, with his comparatively poor stipend, was better off to the extent of £50 a year which was the annuity Maria brought with her on their marriage, a settlement made presumably for her own use on the death of both her parents some few years before. There was no question then of divided properties. It all went into the common pool which, in spite of what is now upheld by freedom fighters in the cause of Women's Liberation is by far the best arrangement for your average chauvinistic male pig.

Patrick was anything but, of course, for he had never enough money to spend on self-gratification apart from what necessarily had to be dispersed in providing for an over-large family. But the little extra was doubly welcome in making more habitable the roomy parsonage that was

Clough House; a great deal more comfortable too. When at day's end and the completion of his church duties he trudged up Clough Lane it was to be greeted from afar by the warm glow of firelight in the parlour window of his own parsonage and his faithful little wife Maria endlessly sewing . . . shirts, sheets, handkerchiefs . . . "oceans of needlework" as Charlotte was later to refer to her own labours as a governess. There was no popping out then to Marks & Spencer or the handy little draper's shop on the corner.

Patrick would then settle down to the writing of his poems and sermons and Maria of necessity would adopt the role of patient listener to his long-winded effusions with, no doubt, a wry smile playing about the corners of her lips as she stitched and stitched. Occasionally they visited old friends as far afield as Dewsbury, drinking from other peoples' tea-cups as a welcome change from their own. A pleasant, uneventful existence you might say, but from our point of view how unbelievably dull and boring.

☆   ☆ ☆   ☆

In Leeds, where I found myself a day or two later, I managed to pick up a book which contained extracts from some of those poems of Patrick's. Over a period of seven years (from 1811 to 1818) he published three small volumes of them, together with a couple of prose tales. In fact, everything he wrote was indigestibly 'prosy'. One can well pity poor Maria, a captive audience of one, being compelled to listen to the following for instance:
"The King who sits upon his throne,
And calls the kneeling world his own
Has oft of cares a greater load
Than he who feels his iron rod."
I quote only four lines of the 265 that comprised his "Winter-Night Meditation" from "Cottage Poems" (1811). To be sure, Mr Bronte had no illusions about them and indeed confessed that he had no other intention than to write simple poems for simple people. Who shall say that he did not succeed in that respect. One can only wonder

what Maria really thought about them and was in no position to make known.

Certainly his children never expressed any opinion on their father's work. They simply settled for showing him how it should best be done.

☆   ☆ ☆   ☆

Chapter 9

THORNTON, YORKSHIRE (1815 - 1820)

I GOT OFF the bus from Bradford right opposite Industry and Commercial Streets in the straggling village of Thornton. The tall spire of the parish church of St. James on the main road was indication enough that here my quest was at an end. My quest was to track down the Brontes.

At first glance there seemed little to attract a "foreigner" there, more especially one from the Metropolis. But from maps and guide books I had a fair idea where Thornton's particular treasure lay hid. I crossed the road and walked through the cobbled alleyway that was Industry as opposed to Commerce. There was no visible sign of either.

Market Street, into which both led, was a different proposition altogether. Nothing could more aptly describe this area of neat little shops and hen-picking Monday morning shoppers. This was undoubtedly the bustling centre of Thornton's workaday life, something the to-and-from Bradford traveller on the by-passing main road might well have been unaware of.

I called in the local post-office for stamps and picture postcards as a reminder to distant foreign relations that I was still on the map, though maybe a bit off-centre. "If it's Bronte 'ouse you're looking for it's just round t'corner across roard," a buxom lady informed me. Did I look *that* "foreign" then that I stood out like a visitor from Heckmondwike or Halifax? Indeed, it struck me that the people here were so much a race apart that even neighbouring Bradford was a kind of No-man's land into which one penetrated only from the dire necessity of earning a living.

So completely absorbed everyone seemed in his own particular train of thoughts that I couldn't help wondering

if they subscribed here to the traditional attitude of
Haworth folk, once described so graphically by Charlotte
Bronte to her biographer, Mrs Gaskell: "Keep a stone in
thy pocket seven years; turn it, and keep it seven years
longer, that it may be ever ready to thine hand when thine
enemy draws near." If you want a parallel, think of old
Joseph in "Wuthering Heights".

☆   ☆ ☆   ☆

Charlotte was born "in t' parsonage 'ouse across roard"
in April 1816. So too were Branwell, Emily and Anne in
the course of the next four years. It says much for what
frail and delicate Maria Branwell from the semi-tropical
climate of Penzance had to endure in the matter of child-
bearing that she had already given birth to little Maria and
Elizabeth up at Hightown in Hartshead in the two years
prior to her husband's appointment as Thornton's minister.
It was the lot of the poor and the lower middle classes to
be almost continually confined in that way, and the wives
of indigent clergymen were no exception to the general
rule. That Mrs Bronte should finally have succumbed to
an internal cancer was something completely unforeseen.
With her the constant pangs of child-birth would seem to
have been shrugged off like the measles, mumps, or
whooping-cough.

Superficially, No. 25 Market Street looks much as it did
when first occupied by the Bronte family except that the
ground floor parlour of the plain two-storey building has
for some years remained extended and in regular use as a
butcher's shop. It was in this parlour that the four famous
children were born and a wall plaque records the fact. Over
the front door, approached by four stone steps across a
small patch of railed-off garden, a corner stone bears the
legend JAS 1802 as an indication that the house was
formerly the residence of John and Sarah Ashworth.

In a nearby cul-de-sac the boys and girls of Thornton's
Church of England School were whooping it up with
shrieks and cat-calls in their playtime break. Little Maria
and Elizabeth, possibly Charlotte too, may well have

played on the same spot though with far less abandon, much more restraint. Nearer their age-group were the babies at the Nursery School a little further down the road, riding their toy tricycles and tending the dolls in their toy prams.

Market Street here makes a sudden curve into Lower Kipping Lane and then almost nose-dives into the Pinchbeck Valley. One is brought up sharp there, not only by the panoramic view ("Long, low moors, dark with heath, shut in little valleys where a stream waters here and there a fringe of stunted copse" was how Charlotte Bronte described it) but by a quite magnificent old railway viaduct with its graduated arches extending from one sloping green bank to its opposite number.

In neighbouring Kipping House, when the Brontes first arrived in Thornton, lived Mr Firth (a widower) with his only child, 18-year old Elizabeth. It was her cousin, the Rev. Thomas Atkinson, who exchanged livings with Patrick Bronte at Hartshead so that he might be a little nearer Frances Walker, the young lady he eventually married. Socially, Mr and Mrs Bronte benefited a great deal from this fortunate turn of events. They became very friendly with Miss Firth and her circle of acquaintances and there are frequent references in Elizabeth's diary to the "taking of tea" with the minister and his wife at the Market Street parsonage or at Kipping House.

Nearby is the old barn where the local Dissenters, including Joseph and his son "Accepted" Lister once preached before it was abandoned for the 'new' Kipping Chapel, already flourishing when the Brontes arrived in 1815. A passer-by casually informed me that there was a Demolition Order on this historic landmark, but I refused to credit the possibility of such vandalism.

☆   ☆ ☆   ☆

I wandered down "Bronte Old Road" past "Bronte Place" through Thornton's extended New Estate of prim little villas and flats and came at last to the 'new' (1870) church of St. James. On the way a white-haired old lady (obviously as enthusiastic about the Brontes as the local lads are with the progress of Leeds United or Huddersfield) was at pains to point out what I should find there. In particular I was to look out for the Bronte font from the Old Bell Chapel in which Charlotte, Emily, Anne and Branwell were baptised; also the "Bronte Memorial Organ" of 1897, built at a cost of £1,200 from money raised by local working men (something I couldn't imagine any of them doing nowadays). Unfortunately I found neither font nor organ. The church was padlocked and bolted on all sides, as right and tight as the Bank of England.

My informant had told me also that I was on no account to miss the crumbling remains of the Old Bell Chapel (where Mr Bronte was Minister from 1815 to 1820) in the graveyard on the opposite side of the road. At imminent risk to life and limb from the constant stream of cars and lorries on the Bradford highroad (there was no pavement to speak of on that side) I endeavoured to find a way in through the low surrounding brick wall. A small and rusty iron gate eventually gave me access to the enclosure, but progress beyond a yard or two was quite impossible. The coarse grass and weeds grew almost waist-high and there was no sign of a beaten pathway between the sunken graves (which I had been given to understand included that of Joseph and his son "Accepted" Lister). Outside the Malayan jungle I don't ever recollect seeing such a wilderness.

There may well be a Demolition Order on the Dissenters' Old Barn, for 20th Century vandalism and/or neglect was surely never more apparent than in this once sacred spot. Observing that one gable-end, all that remained of the ruined Old Bell Chapel, I couldn't help wondering if, in truth, Thornton deserved to be the birthplace of the immortal Bronte sisters. It would seem to be left to Haworth to attract visitors from all over the civilised world who might otherwise be persuaded to think the Parsonage House on Market Street at least of comparative importance.

☆   ☆ ☆   ☆

Chapter 10

HAWORTH, YORKSHIRE (April 1820 - July 1824)

IN HER biographical study of Charlotte Bronte, Mrs Gaskell had this to say about Keighley: "As the gable-ended houses, which intrude themselves corner-wise on the widening street, fall vacant, they are pulled down to allow of greater space for traffic, and a more modern style of architecture. The quaint and narrow shop-windows of fifty years ago are giving place to large panes and plate-glass."

She might have been writing about any town or village today except that this introductory chapter dates from the latter end of 1855.

Keighley is some four miles from Haworth and what Mrs Gaskell found new-fangled about it then might well strike us as being still delightfully rural and old-fashioned in spite of its industrial background. For instance, she mentions the railway station as being a quarter of a mile from the town. When you descend from a train there now you find yourself bang in the middle of a thriving commercial centre with high-rise office blocks and one of the finest supermarkets anywhere in the West Riding.

To reach Haworth from Keighley you can take either bus or train unless you have a car or are bent on walking (which was the Brontes' more regular form of transport). British Rail abandoned their link with the past at the end of 1961 but some half-a-dozen years later the line was taken over by the Keighley and Worth Valley Preservation Society, a voluntarily-run organisation of local business men and their enthusiastic supporters. They are prepared to transport you over a 15 mile circuit of track behind a real live steam locomotive, one of the many they have collected from all over the country and dressed up in their original company liveries. It was this same stretch of track which was used in the filming of E. Nesbit's little classic,

"The Railway Children".

If you elect to go by bus (and they are, or were, quite frequent) you will be travelling through much the same surroundings as described by Mrs Gaskell: "The town of Keighley", she says, "never quite melts into country on the road to Haworth, although the houses become more sparse as the traveller journeys upwards to the grey round hills that seem to bound his journey in a westerly direction." It is not that much changed now except in the matter of sparsity. The "villas, great worsted factories and rows of workmen's houses" she speaks of have extended themselves at the expense of the "old-fashioned farmhouses and outbuildings" she also noted. But she is still dead right in some particulars. For the traveller on this road, Haworth village can still be seen two miles before arrival — "situated on the side of a pretty steep hill, with a background of dun and purple moors, rising and sweeping away yet higher than the church, which is built at the very summit of the long narrow street." The road still "appears to turn away from Haworth as it winds round the base of the shoulder of a hill" before "it crosses a bridge over the 'beck' and the ascent through the village begins . . ."

It was up this steep ascent, one stormy April day in 1820, that seven carts laden with the furniture and effects of the Bronte family slowly lumbered en route from Thornton to the Parsonage House adjacent to the moorland church of St. Michael and all Angels.

☆   ☆ ☆   ☆

It must have been quite a remarkable procession and one is tempted to wonder how the good people of Haworth ("independent, wilful, and full of grim humour") reacted to it. There could have been no escaping the sight and sound of those carts, for as Mrs Gaskell described the village at that time (and it has altered very little since) "The flag-stones . . ." which paved the whole area were "placed end-ways, in order to give a better hold to the horses' feet, and, even with this help, they seem to be in constant danger of slipping backwards.'

What must have intrigued the villagers even more was the light covered wagon which headed this strange caval-cade, led by the striking figure of their new minister and containing his young wife, two teenage servant girls, and the six tiny Bronte children (the oldest, Maria, then only six; the youngest, Anne, still but a baby in arms). The carrier who hired out these carts is said to have remarked to one of his friends that the children were indeed so small he "could have put them all under a clothes basket."

"Poor little mites . . ." may well have been how the women of the neighbourhood summed them up. It probably helped in predisposing them to accept the new minister whose 'posting' to their parish had at first been so stubbornly resisted. For some time now the Vicar of Bradford had been made responsible for such appoint-ments, but the people of Haworth claimed a more ancient right to elect their own parson. It dated back to the Reformation and was supported by the fact that the local freeholders and trustees had control of the land rents and tithes from which most of the incumbent's stipend was paid. They had already harassed the previous minister, a Mr Redhead, out of an appointment they considered unjustly foisted upon them, first rising in a body and stamping out of his church in loud-ringing clogs, then confronting him in his pulpit with a drunken local sweep. Finally, he had been forced to flee the parish, literally in danger of life and limb.

How Patrick Bronte finally won over the church elders to accept his nomination says much for his powers of persuasion. On that April day they were at least prepared to take him on trust, though if he eventually succeeded in winning their respect he can never be said to have basked in their affection. He was not that sort of man and they were certainly not that sort of people.

☆   ☆ ☆   ☆

The first time I visited Haworth was a Sunday in summer and the crowd, whose main objective was to get into the Parsonage House Museum, was not unlike what you would expect to see at that time of year promenading the foreshore at Brighton or Blackpool. It did not surprise me to read somewhere later that in any one year not far short of 100,000 people can be expected to flock there from all over the civilised world.

Though not exactly as the Brontes (or Mrs Gaskell) knew it, the general plan of the Parsonage House is much the same as described in Chapter III of the famous biography. "An oblong stone house, facing down the hill on which the village stands, and with the front door right opposite to the western door of the church, distant about a hundred yards . . . The graveyard goes round house and garden, on all sides but one . . . The house consists of four rooms on each floor, and is two storeys high."

Since being taken over as a museum by the Bronte Society in August 1928 some extensions have been made to the original structure in addition to the north and west wing previously added in 1872 by the then incumbent, the Rev. John Wade, who was also responsible for the re-building of the church, the tower of which only was allowed to remain. It seems he was not a little irritated by the reputation bestowed upon the place by his predecessor; maybe, not unjustly.

You pay your money at the door through which this immortal family passed and repassed in the course of their quiet existence and through which all but Anne were carried to their last resting place under the flag-stones and the barn-like roof of the old church. The admission charge was 20p when I was last there and I was able to obtain only an occasional glimpse of the exhibits there owing to the continual pressure of the crowd behind and around me. In the parlour (actually Mr Bronte's study) some of his personal possessions, including his spectacles, his pipe and tobacco-box and an open bible, were grouped together on a central table as though he had merely left them for a moment or two. In the dining-room, just across the entrance hall, was the sofa on which poor Emily died and the old-fashioned upright piano at which both she and her sister Anne so often sat down to play. The kitchen, behind the parlour, contained a fascinating collection of domestic and culinary equipment among which was a salt-box, a pair of scales, toasting and crimping irons, and (most intriguing of all) some of the actual china off which the family dined.

At the top of the stone staircase, which curves gracefully at the point where Mr Bronte nightly wound up the grandfather clock before retiring, are the four bedrooms used at various times by the children, their parents, their aunt Elizabeth Branwell, and Tabitha Aykroyd (their beloved old servant). Work-boxes (containing needles and thread), Emily's writing desk, Charlotte's going-away dress (after her marriage to Mr Nicholls), some of their brother Branwell's crude paintings, their aunt's own particular teapot . . . these can all be seen and are quite breathtaking.

Apart from the fine collection of juvenile manuscripts in the Bonnell extension to the old parsonage I was most struck by the little room on the landing over the front porch which was first used as the children's nursery and later by Emily herself. Traces of the tiny pencilled drawings made by the young Brontes can still be seen on the distempered wall and I understand some of their toys were discovered under the floor-boards there.

I would strongly advise your visiting the museum on a week-day when other enthusiasts are not quite so thick on the ground and the staircase. And more than one visit is definitely called for. There is too much to be taken in at a mere cursory glance.

☆   ☆ ☆   ☆

It was a far less cheerful prospect that greeted poor Mrs Bronte and her precious (and precocious) little family when they descended from the leading wagon on that April day well over 150 years ago. A bare stone house . . . bare damp floors . . . There was no strip-lighting, no central heating then, though to be sure someone from the village had been deputed to light at least one fire in the rusty old barred grates.

"Been in this place nigh on seventy years," an old

Haworth inhabitant once informed me, "and ain't set foot in that there parsonage 'ouse, not once. They should spend more time looking after the living than worriting about the dead." I have a feeling that Mrs Bronte must have had much the same aversion towards it on first acquaintance, though for a more compelling reason. She had to live in it, after all.

Certainly, insofar as she was concerned, it never was exactly what you might call a home. Mr Bronte was no doubt well satisfied, so long as the domestic arrangements ran smoothly and in any case he must have considered his removal there a step in the right direction. But it could have been no life at all for the children, more especially when their mother was first struck down by the internal cancer from which she died and had necessarily to be shut off from their company in a silent sick-room. Mrs Gaskell reports an old woman who nursed the minister's wife as saying that "You would not have known there was a child in the house, they were such still, noiseless, good little creatures. Maria" (aged seven at the time) "would shut herself up in the children's study with a newspaper, and be able to tell one everything when she came out; debates in parliament, and I don't know what all." She used to think them spiritless, she said, they were so different to any children she had ever seen. Recalling my own children's noisy prattle I can't help wondering how I would have reacted to something so unnatural. Maria, in particular, for all that she was "as good as a mother to her sisters and brother" strikes me as rather an oddity, if not a downright little prig.

Mr Bronte, as would appear to be his normal custom, shut himself away in his study for long periods and more often than not took his meals on his own. If only little Branwell, his ill-fated son, had been allowed occasionally to beat loudly on a toy drum . . . how different things might have been for all of them. He must often have felt like doing so, the only boy among all those clever little girls.

As it was, the only recreation they appear to have had was to walk out hand in hand together on the moors;

never (or hardly ever) in the opposite direction, down through the cobble-stoned village. "They kept themselves to themselves" was the general opinion the Haworth folk had of their minister and his family. On only one occasion are the children reported as having attended a party in the village. They are said to have left early, not being able to understand, or comprehend, any of the games being played there.

☆   ☆ ☆   ☆

Poor Mrs Bronte died on September 15th 1821 (in the 39th year of her age) leaving 'the folk who lived on the hill' more isolated than ever, if one can conceive such a thing possible. Mr Bronte, thereafter, came out of his shell at least to the extent of making himself personally responsible for his children's education. The domestic arrangements of the household he left in the firm and capable hands of his sister-in-law, Elizabeth Branwell, who spent most of her time 'clicking' up and down the flag-stone floors bemoaning the fact that in duty bound she had been called on to exchange the warm social climate of her native Penzance for Haworth's comparative hell on earth and that mainly because Mr Bronte had been unable to persuade anyone to take on the role of second wife and mother to his "small, but sweet family". She too spent the greater part of the day shut up in her own bedroom where she occasionally instructed the older girls in how best to cope with "oceans of needlework . . . yards of cambric to hem . . . muslin nightcaps to make . . ." as Charlotte was later to complain of another taskmaster in a not dissimilar situation.

Possibly these enforced tasks (necessarily disrupting the even tenor of their ways) made both Mr Bronte and Aunt Branwell a little more irritable than was their normal custom. In any case, the older children (in particular) had need to be stretched educationally some way beyond what they felt themselves capable of, more especially if they were to make their own way in life (than which nothing was more certain). Opportunely at that time (Maria was

then 11 years old) a leaflet came into Mr Bronte's posses-
sion advertising the fact that a school had been opened,
for the prime purpose of educating the daughters of
indigent clergymen, at a small hamlet called Cowan Bridge,
on the coach-road between Leeds and Kendal. This establishment was under the control of a rather puritanical but
philanthropic gentleman, the Rev. William Carus Wilson,
who was prepared to take at least the most likely of Mr
Bronte's small charges off his hands for the almost derisory
fee of £14 a year for each pupil, plus an optional £3 for
music, drawing, etc.

After careful consideration and some detailed calcul-
ation Mr Bronte decided to avail himself of this heaven-
sent opportunity. In July 1824 Maria and her younger
sister Elizabeth were both enrolled at this school. Charlotte
and Emily followed them in the autumn of the same year.

Next to his marriage this was the most fatal decision
Mr Bronte was called upon to make in the course of his
long life. It turned out to be even more disastrous.

☆   ☆ ☆   ☆

Chapter 11

INTERLUDE – COWAN BRIDGE
(July 1824 - June 1825)

SOME PEOPLE incline to dismiss "Jane Eyre" as a lot of romantic nonsense and certainly those chapters which deal with Jane's off and on again love affair with Mr Rochester would appear to imply a great deal of wishful thinking on the part of Charlotte Bronte when she wrote them and seemed likely to remain so for the rest of her unnatural life.

In the world of fiction nothing sells better than romance, of course, and Charlotte's first published novel was a phenomenal success from the start. What particularly attracted and (in some cases) repelled the reading public of 1847 was the scandal attaching to the liaison between an unsophisticated governess and her employer, a married man and in every sense a man of the world, saddled irrevocably with a lunatic wife. This touch of the macabre, one might almost say the downright melodramatic, was added spice to an already highly seasoned emotional mixture. One literally could not put the book down, having once taken it up, and it continues to remain as thoroughly absorbing from first page to last.

It must be acknowledged, however, that the greater part of "Jane Eyre" bears testimony only to what the unbridled imagination is capable of when allowed to run riot. It is the triumph of the fanciful over the feasible and as much part of a make-believe world as the stories of Hans Andersen and Charles Perrault. Jane is a 19th century Cinderella and Rochester her fairy prince. It is a tradition which has persisted through such highly emotive periodical literature as "Bow Bells" and "Peg's Paper" down to certain women's magazine stories of our so-called sophisticated times.

The difference with "Jane Eyre", however, apart from its being so much better written, is the fact that it relates also to the dark world of the Brothers Grimm. When Charlotte chooses, for all too short a date, to write directly out of her own experience, we get the much more plausible account of what befell her little orphan heroine under instruction at Lowood School. This, for the majority of modern readers, is by far the most gripping part of the whole book, because the most true to life as Charlotte actually lived it. Lowood School, in fact, was so realistic a counterpart to that educational establishment for the daughters of indigent clergymen at Cowan Bridge which Charlotte herself attended that it was immediately recognised as such by those of her contemporaries who had gone through the same soul-shattering experience.

☆   ☆ ☆   ☆

I, myself, can vividly recall travelling on the A65 from Leeds to Kendal via Guiseley, Skipton, Settle and Ingleton, having previously driven up from London through the better part of the daylight hours. It was near the crack of dawn when I entered that region described so graphically by little Jane Eyre herself on her first approach to the Institution of Lowood: "Great grey hills heaved up round the horizon; as twilight deepened, we descended a valley, dark with wood . . ." But for the time of day, or rather night, my first impression of the immediate neighbourhood was pretty much the same.

I was quite as fatigued as she must have been after her 50-mile coach journey from the Red Room at Gateshead, or as Charlotte herself on a similar journey from Haworth via Keighley in the late summer of 1824. In my case, however, there was not the same sense of foreboding at journey's end that both Charlotte and Jane must have felt, no grim dormitory waiting with its "long rows of beds, each of which quickly filled with two occupants", or, at that same unearthly hour "a rushlight or two" burning and "one basin to six girls, on the stands down the middle of the room" grudgingly provided for pre-breakfast

ablutions. I was confidently expecting the comfort of a
modestly decent hotel in Kendal where, if my first meal of
the day was to include porridge, it would not be so dis-
gustingly burnt as at either Lowood or Cowan Bridge and
dinner would not consist of a mess of "indifferent
potatoes and strange shreds of rusty meat" served up "in
two huge tinplated vessels, whence rose a strong steam
redolent of rancid fat."

I was tired, that's all. Indeed, I had been almost lulled
to sleep by the hypnotic effect those metal-studded
"cat's-eyes" have on all long-distance travellers when
viewed from the windscreen of a car at night on those
constantly twisting moorland roads. For the space of
some thirty minutes I endeavoured to snatch a Churchillian
rest period in a convenient lay-by, but was soon stiff in
every joint and quite literally blue with cold. I decided to
push on the fourteen or so odd miles remaining to complete my journey.

It was then, on making a sharp right-hand turn over one
of those 'becks' which are such a prominent feature of that
part of the country, that I first caught sight of the metal
name-plate at the side of the road and the group of low-
lying cottages at right-angles to it. In that completely
unexpected way I had stumbled on "Cowan Bridge", of
immortal memory.

☆   ☆ ☆   ☆

There was little to explore, even in broad daylight,
though I might have observed then what I missed in the
wee small hours – the plaque on the gable-end of one of
the converted dwelling-houses which informed the passer-
by that "At this school Maria, Elizabeth, Charlotte, Emily,
daughters of the Rev. P. Bronte were educated in 1824-
25."

The bare bones of what remained had of necessity to be
clothed with imagination. What any Bronte-lover cannot
but help treat as holy ground seemed at that time of the
morning as blank and empty as an abandoned barrack
square with not a sentry or bugler in sight anywhere. Gone

was the garden with its "covered verandah on one side" and its "broad walks bordering a middle space divided into scores of little beds" for the cultivation of which each little allotment-holder had been made personally responsible. There was no sign of any of the school's small pupils dressed in their "brown stuff frocks of quaint fashion, and long holland pinafores" and all wearing "woollen stockings and country-made shoes fastened with brass buckles."

The Rev. William Carus Wilson (alias Mr Brocklehurst) that "black pillar" with the "grim face at the top, like a carved mask" would obviously not be carrying out one of his periodical inspections today, I could not help reflecting. No longer (in the words of Mrs Gaskell) would "his love of authority" lead to so much "unnecessary and irritating meddling with little matters." He sleeps somewhere, smugly conscious that the greater part of the work he undertook was carried out with good intent even if some people chose to interpret things otherwise.

After all, the fee of £14 per annum charged to hard-up parsons for the education of their female offspring, even though supplemented by private subscriptions, barely covered the overhead costs of running the establishment which, in consequence, was little more than a charitable institution. "Plain fare, simple attire, unsophisticated accommodation, hardy and active habits" were of necessity the order of the day. The provision of the most trifling of luxuries was not to be encouraged, even if seen fit by the staff. The Rev. Carus Wilson was, in any case, the last person on earth one could appeal or complain to in such matters.

Had he not written in that "penny dreadful" published monthly at Kirkby Lonsdale — "How dreadful is the wickedness of many children, who seem ripe at an early age for every act of sin which they are capable of performing . . ."? So puritanical a person might almost be forgiven for overlooking the fact that domestic arrangements at Cowan Bridge left much to be desired and in particular that the cook employed there (a personal friend of long standing) was dirty, careless, and wasteful in preparing the comparatively good food provided. It is the way of all self-centred, narrow-minded zealots.

Other conditions too served to bring on the "low fever" which swept through and decimated the school in the Spring of 1825. In Chapter IX of "Jane Eyre" Charlotte refers to the "forest-dell, where Lowood lay" as being "the cradle of fog and fog-bred pestilence; which, quickening with the quickening spring, crept into the Orphan Asylum, breathed typhus through its crowded school-room and dormitory, and, ere May arrived, transformed the seminary into an hospital."

Charlotte had every reason to be fiercely partisan on this issue, more especially when dealing with the death of little Helen Burns, that slovenly, careless, long-suffering and exceedingly intelligent child who was in some ways so like her own elder sister, Maria. They buried Helen in Brocklebridge (actually Tunstall) churchyard, to which the children were made to walk two miles every Sunday for morning and afternoon services "setting out cold and arriving colder". Maria was sent home to die at Haworth in early May. Elizabeth, the second of the Bronte children, followed her to the grave little more than a month later.

By the grace of God, Charlotte and Emily were spared us on that occasion, if only for a few more tragic years. Otherwise there would have been no "Jane Eyre", no "Wuthering Heights", no permanent record of the Rev. Patrick Bronte and his remarkable family ever having passed this way.

☆   ☆ ☆   ☆

It was just as well I met no other traveller on the road to Kendal in the early morning light of that memorable day. The confused state of my mind after regretfully leaving Cowan Bridge behind me would have boded no good to anyone else at the wheel of a car. I was indeed thankful to arrive at my destination without having spilled over into a ditch or wrapped myself round the trunk of a tree.

Reflecting later in the bar-parlour of a lakeside hotel, I

got into conversation with some local worthy who assured me that Lowood/Cowan Bridge School was still in existence. "It's up at Casterton now," he said, "and a quite excellent school too, from what I've heard of it."

It might well be, I thought. But if a hard school is what genius needs to flower and flourish in I am rather doubtful if another Charlotte or Emily Bronte will emanate from that quarter. Certainly "Jane Eyre" and "Catherine Earnshaw" would never have survived on anything but burnt porridge and rusty meat.

☆   ☆ ☆   ☆

Chapter 12

INTERLUDE – THE COVE, SILVERDALE, LANCS.
(1 June 1825)

MRS GASKELL seems to have been under the impression that Charlotte and Emily returned to Cowan Bridge School after the deaths of their two elder sisters. Indeed, she states categorically that they went back there "after the Midsummer holidays in this fatal year" (1825) though "before the next winter, it was thought desirable to advise their removal . . . as it was evident that the damp situation of the house . . . did not suit their health."

On the face of it this is patently absurd. Though Charlotte's biographer was sometimes inclined to portray Mr Bronte in the most unfavourable light it is too much to conceive that he could possibly have entertained such an idea in the light of all that had happened. One is inclined to wonder that Mrs Gaskell should have accepted it so easily whether tacitly, or from not being told otherwise (as was too often the case), or from not troubling to verify as fact what had been presented to her in the form of idle gossip.

It was a fault in her that she failed to get at the roots of much that now seems quite inexplicable to us in the general character of the Bronte children and in particular of Mr Bronte himself. For instance, it seems more than remarkable to me that no mention is ever made of any of Patrick's innumerable Irish relations having attended his wife's funeral or the funeral of any one of his six children (to say nothing of Charlotte's wedding). Nor would he appear to have been present at the graveside of his own father or mother. Indeed, Mrs Gaskell would seem to imply that after his ordination in the Church of England and his first appointment to Wethersfield in Essex all communication with his family in County Down, or elsewhere in the world, was cut off completely.

We do know, from later researches into the family's history, that Mr Bronte made an annual allowance to his mother and that this must have been something of a strain on his meagre financial resources. All honour to him for that. But that he should otherwise have not wished to acknowledge their existence seems a far more damning condemnation of his character than any of the eccentricities and wild outbursts of temper Mrs Gaskell showed no restraint in portraying. That she should have preserved a discreet silence with regard to the early years of his ministry (in particular where it concerned his thwarted love affair with Mary Burder) is understandable in view of the embarrassment it might well have caused in that quarter. She observed no such tact, however, in her dealings with the Rev. Carus Wilson of Cowan Bridge and Mrs Robinson of Thorp Green (Branwell's supposed mistress), threatened though she was later on both counts with possible court action. The point is that Mrs Gaskell was in a better position than any subsequent biographer to obtain the truth of much that puzzles us direct from the horse's mouth, so to speak, and for some reason or other she signally failed to do so.

One is led to the conclusion that Mr Bronte was in some ways ashamed of his peasant origins (there is a hint of this in his dealings with Mary Burder) though there would seem no reason why he should be. Indeed, from what I have myself discovered in that direction most of his Irish forbears and descendants seem to have done pretty well for themselves in later life. His brothers William, Hugh, James and Walsh all lived (like himself) to be over 80, though if there was a weakness in this respect it would appear (as with his own immediate family) to have been on the distaff side. His sister Jane, for instance, died when she was only 31, and none of his own children reached middle-age. Only one of Patrick's five sisters ever married and she died without issue. There is a direct parallel here with his own five daughters. Only Charlotte, among them, was led to the altar and she too died before her child could be born.

Two only of Patrick's brothers, William and Walsh,

married and had descendants. Some of these settled later in America and the family is still flourishing there now, to the best of my knowledge. One of Walsh Bronte's sons was drowned "when fording the river Bann" on 22 September 1833 when he was only 22. Charlotte was then 17 years old but no mention is made anywhere of the death of this young cousin, certainly not by Patrick or Mrs Gaskell. It is interesting to reflect that a grandson of brother William served in the Crimea and that two daughters of another grandson were christened, respectively, Charlotte and Anne.

☆ ☆ ☆ ☆

It's a great pity that some generations of Bronte enthusiasts were not informed about Silverdale and that either Mrs Gaskell knew nothing about it or was never tempted to probe further into the matter. Could Mr Bronte possibly have forgotten?

It was left to a later biograpaher, Winifred Gerin, to establish the fact that it was to The Cove, at Silverdale, on Morecambe Bay, that Charlotte and Emily were sent as children after the outbreak of fever at Cowan Bridge School and that from there they were brought back to Haworth by their father on 1st June 1825.

So far as can be ascertained they spent only one night in the Rev. Carus Wilson's seaside home there, but the occasion was sufficiently remarkable for the back bedroom in which they slept to be designated "The Bronte Room" in the hostel for old and handicapped people which the erstwhile Cove has become today.

I recall, some time ago, being left to kick my heels for some evening hours in nearby Heysham whilst waiting for the late night boat to Belfast. I set off walking idly by the sea (the Irish Sea, in fact) and in just over an hour or so found myself on the margin of Morecambe Bay, than which there are few more picturesque or entrancing. It was late summer and I was treated to the spectacle of one of the most fantastic sunsets it has ever been my good fortune to witness. Not for nothing did Turner make it the subject of several of his paintings. Nobody had a better eye for the colourful interplay of light and shade on sea and sky.

I knew nothing of The Cove at that time or I most certainly would have made the attempt to go further in that direction. It was just as well I didn't really, since Silverdale is at least seven miles from Morecambe, on the other side of the Bay. Quite impossible in the time I had at my disposal, to say nothing of the fact that I would have missed my boat if I had taken on such a roundabout journey. Maybe I might have ended up sufficiently handicapped to claim a night's lodging in that excellent institution, preferably in the immortal Bronte Room itself.

And insofar as it concerned Mrs Gaskell it seems even more remarkable that she should have been a frequent visitor to the neighbourhood, writing several of her stories there and watching Morecambe's celebrated sunsets from the castellated tower of Gibraltar (one of the most prominent features of Silverdale's landscape).

She would have kicked herself could she have known about The Cove and the Bronte children's night's lodging there. Or did she discover the fact later and choose to say nothing about it on that account?

☆　　☆ ☆　　　☆

Chapter 13

HAWORTH (June 1825 - January 1831)

THE LAST TIME I was in Leeds (in a sports and games shop) my wife had the temerity to ask for a Chelsea football pennant . . . She is not a football fan; neither am I, exactly. But my small grandson most decidedly is.

While I waited for her, I couldn't help toying with the idea that on one of his occasional visits to the city Mr Bronte may well have purchased in this particular area (if not in this particular shop) that box of wooden soldiers for his son, Branwell, which was so substantially to alter the lives of the Bronte children. Fantastic and utterly nonsensical thought, of course. Leeds has been built on and built on again and again since then.

"I have had a curious packet confided to me," wrote Mrs Gaskell in her biography of Charlotte, "containing an immense amount of manuscript, in an inconceivably small space; tales, dramas, poems, romances, written principally by Charlotte, in a hand which it is almost impossible to decipher without the aid of a magnifying glass." In August 1830, Charlotte herself catalogued a list of such 'plays' (as she called them) covering a period of just under 18 months. "Making" (she says) "in the whole twenty-two volumes." She was then only 14 years old.

I have seen some of these "volumes" in the Parsonage House Museum at Haworth. Each volume contains between 60 and 100 pages, the page sizes being on average approximately 2" long by 1½" across and the separate volumes stitched together in that coarse type of brown and blue paper in which sugar and currants were usually packed. The hand-printed words on each page are so minute and the lines so tightly compressed in the available space that it must indeed have been as impossible to write them as to read them without strain. No wonder Charlotte, in particular, was so short-sighted!

Mrs Gaskell (possibly with "Jane Eyre" and "Wuthering Heights" in mind) seems disposed to regard the greater part of this early work as "juvenilia", the sort of thing any intelligent child might be expected to produced during long periods of uninterrupted leisure. I have seen work of a similar kind done by children of my own acquaintance during the period immediately after the first World War and I would like to believe it is still being produced somewhere in secret. It was left to a later biographer, however, (Fanny E. Ratchford in "The Brontes' Web of Childhood", New York 1941) to examine these early writings with any degree of thoroughness and understanding and to prove by detailed analysis just how remarkable some of them really were.

Indeed, without this early workshop practice it is doubtful if the later novels and poems would ever have been written. Nothing of lasting value is ever built unless some prentice hand has first got to grips with the initial blue-prints.

☆   ☆ ☆   ☆

"Papa bought Branwell some wooden soldiers at Leeds" wrote Charlotte in one of her self-explanatory papers of that time — "when papa came home it was night, and we were in bed, so next morning Branwell came to our door with a box of soldiers. Emily and I jumped out of bed, and I snatched up one and exclaimed, "This is the Duke of Wellington! This shall be the Duke!" When I said this Emily likewise took one up and said it should be hers; when Anne came down, she said one should be hers. Mine was the prettiest of the whole, and the tallest, and the most perfect in every part. Emily's was a grave-looking fellow, and we called him "Gravey". Anne's was a queer little thing, much like herself, and we called him "Waiting Boy". Branwell chose his, and called him "Buonaparte". From this incident Charlotte dates the production of their first recorded 'play' — "Young Men" — as June, 1826.

It is interesting to note how the elder sister's dominant

and forceful character is already firmly established in the implied criticism of her two younger sisters. Her soldier was indisputably "the prettiest . . . tallest . . . most perfect in every part". Emily's (how aptly) is "a grave-looking fellow". Anne's, "a queer little thing, *much like herself*". Branwell's choice, though almost deferred to, seems bang on the nail in the light of after events in her brother's life. As the future black sheep of the family it would seem most fitting that he should have picked on "Buonaparte" who had set out to achieve so much and ended up so ignominiously. What a judge of character Charlotte showed herself to be, even at that tender age . . .

And what a remarkable child she was in other respects too. For instance, Mrs Gaskell records that when she was scarcely 13 she drew up a list of painters "whose works I wish to see . . ." It includes Titian, Raphael, Michelangelo, Leonardo da Vinci, Van Dyck, and Rubens. Somewhere along the line she must have read about the works of these great artists (possibly in books borrowed from the Mechanics' Institute Library at Keighley). But where, in the West Riding, would the opportunity have presented itself for a face to face confrontation with any of the masterpieces they produced? As her situation then was at Haworth, and seemed fated to be for the foreseeable future, how could she possibly hope to make any closer acquaintance with them?

☆   ☆ ☆   ☆

Far-ranging as the Bronte children's imagination undoubtedly was, and there is no better evidence of this than in the fantastic world of continents and islands, cities, states, and institutions, which they created between them in the Angrian and the Gondal chronicles, one cannot but wonder from what source they drew their inspiration. As it was, however, they were better placed than most children in this respect, and this in spite (or perhaps because of) their almost complete isolation from the distractions of the outside world.

In the first place one must take into account their Celtic

origins. Patrick Bronte came from Irish peasant stock. His wife was a Cornish-woman. No two regions of the British Isles are more steeped in folk-lore tradition and all the romance and superstition associated with it. It follows, therefore, that both parents must have contributed a great deal to their awareness of the strange 'goings-on' common at that time among the inhabitants of these regions. When Mrs Bronte died (and what a sobering effect that must have had on the children, more especially when followed so soon after by the loss of their two so-beloved sisters) they came under the direct influence of their aunt, Elizabeth Branwell. She, most reluctantly, had come post-haste from Penzance to take over the running of the household in this cold and inhospitable corner of the country. With her, apart from her natural contrariness, she brought a long mulled-over fund of cautionary tales. Her retailing of these was not unaffected by her strict Methodist upbringing and a consequent obsession with sin and its ramifications which sombrely coloured her outlook on life.

To these strong influences must be added the fact that Mr Bronte at all times encouraged his children to read whatever they fancied in the way of books, newspapers, and magazines. "We take two and see three newspapers a week," wrote Charlotte in 1829. "We take the Leeds Intelligencer, Tory, and the Leeds Mercury, Whig . . . We see the John Bull; it is high Tory, very violent. Mr Driver lends us it, as likewise Blackwood's Magazine". One can well imagine what they extracted and reconstructed from this ragbag of information. By comparison they would have got far less to feed their appetites from the more down-to-earth columns of the News of the World and The People.

Perhaps the strongest influence exerted upon the children at that time was that of Tabitha Aykroyd who was engaged as a servant by Mr Bronte after the deaths of little Maria and Elizabeth and the return home from Cowan Bridge School of little Charlotte and Emily. She was already 54 years old when she first came to the Parsonage in 1825 and she was to remain there for another thirty years, dying only a month or two before Charlotte herself. You can see her grave in the old churchyard, close up against the wall dividing it from the Parsonage garden.

To the children she was known affectionately as "Tabby" and treated by them in every way as an equal in the family, nay more — a personal friend and confidante. Mrs Gaskell describes her (with almost the same affection) as "a thorough specimen of a Yorkshire woman of her class, in dialect, in appearance, and in character. She abounded in strong practical sense and shrewdness. Her words were far from flattery; but she would spare no deeds in the cause of those whom she kindly regarded. She ruled the children pretty sharply; and yet never grudged a little extra trouble to provide them with such small treats as came within her power."

Tabby had lived in Haworth all her life and remembered when the pack-horses used to come through the village with their tinkling bells in a bygone age when there were no mills or factories and wool-spinning was done by hand in the neighbouring farmhouses. Much like the peasantry in Patrick Bronte's childhood days she had a fixed belief in fairies and hob-goblins having once frequented the 'becks' and hollows of the surrounding moorland. She had an inexhaustible fund of stories to tell about the strange folk who had once lived in its scattered cottages and isolated mansions and the tragedies, romances, and melo-dramatic happenings that had been a common feature of their everyday working lives.

That the children absorbed these tales like their mother's milk and with much the same effect goes without saying. How much it influenced what they were writing (on the corners of the coarse-grained table in the cosy warmth of the fire-lit kitchen) is quite incalculable. Did Heathcliff spring from that rough but kindly source — or Mr Rochester? How much of old Joseph or Mr Lockwood's garrulous house-keeper, Ellen Dean, came more or less fully-clothed from the lips of that reminiscing old wiseacre? This is something we shall never know and can only debate about till Kingdom Come or the fairies and hob-goblins return to their native 'becks' and hollows.

Chapter 14

INTERLUDE – ROE HEAD, MIRFIELD
(January 1831 - July 1832)

IN JANUARY 1831 Mr Bronte decided that Charlotte's
education should be extended a step or two beyond the
bounds imposed on it by his limited resources at Haworth.
She was then nearly 15 years old and in the natural order
of things (as applicable to that particular period and the
family's straitened circumstances) must soon be expected
to make her own way in the world. His choice (aided and
abetted by some of his old friends at Thornton) fell upon
Roe Head School at Mirfield, described later by Mrs
Gaskell as "a cheerful roomy country house, standing a
little apart in a field, on the right of the road from Leeds
to Huddersfield."

In the words of the one biographer who was in a
position to know and understand her, Charlotte at that
time was "a quiet, thoughtful girl . . . very small in figure"
('stunted' was how she described herself) "with soft, thick,
brown hair, and peculiar eyes . . . They were large, and
well shaped; their colour a reddish brown; but if the iris
was closely examined, it appeared to be composed of a
great variety of tints." Having put the best face on it, so to
speak, Mrs Gaskell goes on to portray the rest of her
features as "plain, large, and ill-set;" However, she qualified this by asserting that "the eyes and power of the
countenance overbalanced every physical defect; the
crooked mouth and the large nose were forgotten, and the
whole face arrested the attention . . . Her hands and feet
were the smallest I ever saw; when one of the former was
placed in mine, it was like the soft touch of a bird in the
middle of my palm."

Mary Taylor, herself a pupil at Roe Head who was later
to become one of Charlotte's closest friends (the other

being Ellen Nussey) describes her first sight of her as "coming out of a covered cart, in very old-fashioned clothes, and looking very cold and miserable . . . She looked a little old woman, so short-sighted that she always appeared to be seeking something, and moving her head from side to side to catch a sight of it . . ."

Some years later she told Charlotte she thought she had been very impertinent in calling her downright ugly, to which Charlotte replied, "You did me a great deal of good, Polly, so don't repent of it."

☆   ☆ ☆   ☆

Roe Head, when Charlotte was first enrolled there, was run by the four Miss Woolers, a group of amiable maiden ladies of whom the presiding genius was Miss Margaret. Charlotte never lost contact with this good friend all her life. Indeed, it was Margaret Wooler who 'gave her away' on the occasion of her marriage to Arthur Bell Nicholls (in the absence of Mr Bronte who, initially, did not approve of the liaison).

In marked contrast to Cowan Bridge the educational establishment at Roe Head was more in the nature of a home from home than a school. The number of pupils never exceeded ten young ladies during Charlotte's stay there and the acquisition of knowledge was pursued for its own sake and as a process of self-enlightenment rather than as a set course of instruction. There was no regular time table or defined classroom procedure. The girls brought their work for Miss Wooler's commendation or correction as and when it was completed, and they were encouraged to continue studying in their so-called 'off-duty' hours rather than to fling pen and paper to the wind on the stroke of a bell. Ample opportunity was provided for recreation and games, anyway, though Mary Taylor's opinion of Charlotte's prowess in that direction was (as usual) blunt and to the point: "Some of us once urged her to be on our side in a game at ball. She said she had never played and could not play. We made her try, but soon found that she could not see the ball, so we put her out."

Charlotte it seems was not to be parted from an open book, even in play hours.

Not that she was regarded as a 'blue stocking' by any means. On first acquaintance, Mary Taylor thought her "very ignorant, for she had never learnt grammar at all, and very little geography." What she knew about literature (especially poetry) soon confounded them all, however. Indeed, she excelled so much in that field (as well as in drawing) that Miss Wooler eventually had just cause to be proud of her as a prize pupil.

Charlotte proved to be very popular among her schoolfellows and never more so than when she regaled them with "horror" stories of her own making in the dormitory at night. "On one occasion," Mrs Gaskell reports, "the effect was such that she was led to scream out loud, and Miss Wooler, coming upstairs, found that one of the listeners had been seized with violent palpitations, in consequence of the excitement produced by Charlotte's story."

This was Charlotte giving full rein to her imagination with a vengeance, much as she was to do later in treating with the mad wife of Mr Rochester, in Jane Eyre. But the practical, down-to-earth side of her nature was apt soon to reassert itself (as in describing Jane's harrowing experience of life at Lowood and in her dramatic reconstruction of the Luddites' attack on Rawfold's Mill, in Shirley). According to Mary Taylor (in the long reminiscent letter she wrote Mrs Gaskell in January 1856) she was always in touch with day to day events as reflected in parliamentary proceedings. "She worshipped the Duke of Wellington" (said Mary) though she was of the opinion that "Sir Robert Peel was not to be trusted; he did not act from principle like the rest, but from expediency." What she would have thought of today's politicians beggars description.

Mary Taylor, of course, was the right sort of girl to spark off reflections of that kind and Charlotte gained immeasurably from contact with her at such an early age. The Taylors were a long established but extremely radical and dissenting family. Mary's father was a manufacturer of wool cloth who, though he gloried in speaking his mind in a strong Yorkshire dialect was equally fluent in French and Italian, having travelled much on the Continent in the course of his business. His wife, on the other hand, was a rather sour and hard-bitten character, not much loved even in the bosom of her family. They had four sons and one other daughter, Martha, who was also a pupil at Roe Head during Charlotte's stay there. She earned the nickname "Boisterous" from her rather madcap ways and was much loved by all who knew her. Sadly, she was to die later in Brussels, being buried in the English cemetery there.

Charlotte drew largely on Mr Taylor's character when portraying Yorke Hunsden in The Professor and Hiram Yorke in Shirley. She used both Martha and Mary in the latter novel, a fact which was immediately recognised by those who knew them and which helped to establish the authorship of both Jane Eyre and Shirley, till then veiled under the pseudonym of "Currer Bell".

One is at some pains, however, to identify Charlotte's other friend, Ellen Nussey, in any of the novels though some have found a faint resemblance to her in the character of Caroline Helstone, daughter of "Shirley's" militant parson. This would appear all the more remarkable when one takes into consideration the fact that Ellen was truly Charlotte's dearest friend throughout the remainder of her life. Indeed, but for the many letters from Charlotte which she insisted on preserving, our knowledge of the Brontes and their household affairs would be sadly lacking, as Mrs Gaskell would have been the first to admit. Mary Taylor, on the other hand, kept none of hers, and we are that much worse off in consequence.

The fact is, of course, that Ellen Nussey was the exact opposite of Mary Taylor in every way. She came from a high Tory family whose members at various times had been court physicians and local magistrates, pillars of the Establishment than whom none could be more antithetical to the Taylors who openly scoffed at so-called pretensions of that kind. In our own day the gap between them would have been as wide as that between the far Right and the extreme Left in local and national politics.

Ellen herself was what one might describe as a "nice" girl, very religious, not very clever, pleasant-looking rather than pretty. An ideal Sunday School teacher in every way and the last to venture an opinion that would put her on any side but that of the angels. We might call her "dull" but to Charlotte she represented something that was lacking in her own nature; stability perhaps. Again and again she consulted her whenever she was vexed in spirit (which was often) or whenever she wanted advice in the form of plain commonsense. Her own summing up of their relationship was that they "suited". It was as simple and straight-forward as that.

How can one put a character of that kind in a novel? All Charlotte's have rough edges, something you can at least get to grips with from the point of view of development. Ellen Nussey was virtually colourless, which is the way of all those of too sweet, too placid a nature. What sells newspapers is bad news. Much the same can be said of any novel powerful enough to grip and hold the reader's attention.

☆   ☆ ☆   ☆

Mirfield is some 20 miles from Haworth and, if one needs to rely on public transport, very difficult of access from that direction (somewhat confusing even by car). We know Charlotte came from thence by the inevitable "covered cart" and quite some time it must have taken her too. All the more credit to her brother, Branwell, who we are given to understand paid a surprise visit to Roe Head School, doing both the outward and return journey on foot! A very short day they must have had together.

I came there via Huddersfield which is approximately half the distance Mary Taylor had to travel from her home at Gomersal (The Red House) and Ellen Nussey from the Rydings, at Birstall. Mirfield itself I found to be a pleasant little market town on the river Calder, surrounded by green and well-wooded hills. There is a quaint old inn here, the Three Nuns, referred to by Mrs Gaskell as being "frequented by fustian-dressed mill-hands from the neighbouring worsted factories." Needless to say, I met none of them. I did find the stone cross, however, known locally as the Dumb Steeple, where the Luddites traditionally met to plan their campaigns of action.

I got rather a shock from my first sight of Roe Head (though I had been prepared for it). The three-storied block with its "old-fashioned semi-circular bow windows" still looks down on the "green slope of pastureland, ending in the pleasant woods of Kirklees" where under a "mouldering stone" Robin Hood is popularly supposed to be buried. But considerable extensions have been made to the original building, in the form of an "L-shaped" block. It is now St. Peter Claver College, one of several such schools run by the Verona Fathers for the training of prospective missionaries. At Mirfield, I learned, the younger boys are provided with a good education up to GCE 'O' level standard and assessed as to their suitability for further advancement in one or other of their establishments centred on London and the Home Counties. They have another training school of the same kind at Dumfries, in Scotland.

I couldn't help wondering what the reaction of Miss Wooler's pupils might have been to the parked cars in the fore-court, the groups of boys sunning themselves on the grass and under the trees and the several motherly-looking women obviously visiting their offspring there that day. Not in Charlotte's wildest imagination could she possibly have conceived anything quite so bizarre. Certainly she may well have been horrified at the mere thought of her old school being under Catholic control. She was never at a loss in expressing what she felt about that particular denomination.

Later that same day, in the bar of a Dewsbury hotel, I got into conversation with a couple of ladies who claimed to have worked on the staff at Roe Head when it was occupied by a local wool manufacturer whose mill, I was given to understand, is still in existence at Mirfield. "It had a huge kitchen," said one of them, "with two of the biggest ranges you ever saw." "Never cared much for the place, myself," said the other. "Always got the impression

THE BRONTËS WERE HERE

you were being watched, even when no-one was about. Quite eerie, sometimes."

Charlotte would have loved that. In her day the unoccupied third floor of Roe Head was supposed to be haunted by a lady whose "rustling silk gown" (according to Mrs Gaskell) "was sometimes heard by the listeners at the foot of the second flight of stairs." It is not on record, however, that anyone ever saw her and Miss Wooler herself scoffed at the very idea.

At nearby Oakwell Hall (later described as "Field Head", Shirley's residence) Mrs Gaskell relates the story of a certain Captain Batt who, one winter evening, "came stalking along the lane, and through the hall, and up the stairs, into his own room, where he vanished. He had been killed in a duel in London that very same afternoon of December 9, 1684.

"They show a bloody footprint there still," she said. I don't know if it is there now, for I never stopped to enquire and wouldn't have had the nerve to do so anyway.

☆   ☆ ☆   ☆

Chapter 15

HAWORTH (July 1832 - July 1835)

AFTER THREE half-yearly terms at Roe Head Charlotte returned to Haworth a little older, much wiser, and with the reward of a silver medal for "Emulation" which was to become part of the stock in trade of the future Parsonage House Museum.

The ensuing three years were comparatively settled and happy ones. For all the Bronte children it can be truly said there was no place quite like home and for the girls, anyway, nothing more satisfying than the regular routine of household chores, varied by reading, writing, and drawing and occasional long walks over the surrounding moors. One of their favourite objectives on these walks was what has come to be known as the "Bronte Falls". You can reach these via West Lane, the village cemetery and the present-day Hill Top Cafe, thence via the road crossing the Lower Laithé Reservoir embankment to the Haworth-Stanbury Road as far as Far Intake. A rough track from here descends to Sladen Beck and the Falls. The journey is just over two miles but well worth the effort (something not taken into account by the Bronte children).

The route is well sign-posted and not too difficult to find. In any case other visitors may well be trekking ahead of you. The Falls themselves are generally no more than a mere trickle through moss-covered rocks but can provide quite a cascade in rainy weather. Of particular interest is the mill-stone grit "Bronte Bridge" crossing the Sladen Beck and the "Bronte Chair", a large stone worn by wind and weather to form a reclining seat, no doubt often occupied by one or other of the children. Incidentally you can proceed by car to Far Intake from whence you need to walk only about a mile, but I feel this is rather a lazy way of making what is otherwise a romantic pilgrimage.

☆   ☆ ☆   ☆

With the added advantage she had received from her schooling at Roe Head Charlotte now took over most of the 'vocational' training of her two younger sisters. Branwell, of course, was already committed to going his own way in this respect. He had for some time been a frequent visitor at the two local inns, The White Lion and The Black Bull, when released from Mr Bronte's efforts to pump a little Greek and Latin into him. Mrs Gaskell records the landlord of The Black Bull as recommending his company "to any chance traveller who might happen to feel solitary or dull over his liquor". "'Do you want some one to help you with your bottle, sir? If you do, I'll send up for Patrick'" (as the villagers called him). Indeed, he was looked on as the life of any party, not merely empty-headed but clever on all counts. "By dint of studying maps," says Mrs Gaskell, "he was well acquainted with it" (i.e. London) "even down to its by-ways, as if he had lived there." It was to stand him in little stead later on when he was to wander aimlessly through those same by-ways with no more definite objective in view than he ever conscientiously set himself to pursue in his native surroundings.

Nevertheless, Charlotte quite literally idolized her brother at that time, though she was to think a great deal less of him later on. For one thing, he was the guiding light in what for her was the thankful resumption of the Angrian Chronicles. His was the administrative genius behind the overall planning of this imaginery African kingdom, down to its last new town and established territory. Charlotte created the social and cultural life of its people, dominated by the infamous Duke of Zamorna with his innumerable intrigues and infidelities; (surely the shadow of Mr Rochester intervened between the candlelight and these reams of close-printed manuscript pages?).

Meanwhile Emily and Anne (of necessity drawn closer together during their sister's absence from the domestic fireside) were exploring their own particular line of country in the Gondal tales whose origins were rooted more firmly in the surrounding hills and moorland of the West Riding. "The Gondals are discovering the interior of Gaaldine" wrote Emily, in her diary paper of 24 Nov 1834. She was literally discovering it with them at the same time as she was peeling the potatoes or busy with other kitchen chores. There was no separation of the real from the imaginary life so far as she was concerned.

☆   ☆ ☆   ☆

"An account of one day is an account of all," (wrote Charlotte to her Roe Head friend, Ellen Nussey, just after her return to Haworth in July 1832). "In the morning, from nine o'clock till half-past twelve, I instruct my sisters, and draw; then we walk till dinner-time. After dinner I sew till tea-time, and after tea I either write, read, or do a little fancy work, or draw, as I please."

Poor Ellen must often have wondered what it was Charlotte was continually "writing" (apart from the correspondence which from that time on they regularly indulged in). Charlotte never took this dearest of friends into her confidence about the "little magazines" that occupied so much of their time though she had made a mention of them to Mary Taylor (at Roe Head) without actually producing anything to satisfy her curiosity. On the other hand she was not backward in putting Ellen's inclinations on the right lines so far as a choice of "reading" was concerned. "If you like poetry" (she wrote) "let it be first-rate; Milton, Shakespeare, Thomson, Goldsmith, Pope (if you will, though I don't admire him), Scott, Byron, Campbell, Wordsworth, and Southey". She made no apology for including Shakespeare and Byron in the same breath, so to speak. "You will know how to choose the good, and to avoid the evil;" (she said) "the finest passages are always the purest, the bad are invariably revolting; you will never wish to read them over twice." One gets the impression she would have 'bowdlerised' them for Ellen's consumption, had it been possible. Mary

Taylor, it goes without saying, could have safely been left to choose for herself.

And "drawing"? It is a fact that during this period (with all the children at home) Mr Bronte engaged William Robinson, an artist from Leeds, to instruct them in the rudiments of that particular accomplishment. But though it gave him over-exaggerated ideas about Branwell's future prospects, it was "no go" so far as Charlotte was concerned. All the sisters were meticulous 'copiers' of plates and mezzotints, but Charlotte, in particular, almost ruined her eyesight in the slow and laborious process.

Branwell, at least, progressed so far as to produce that portrait in oils of the three sisters which is now on view in the National Portrait Gallery, together with a profile of Emily saved from another group portrait that was later destroyed. But for his basking at last in the sisters' reflected glory his work, most certainly, would never have been exhibited there. "Not much better than sign-painting, as to its manipulation," was Mrs Gaskell's caustic comment, "but the likenesses were, I should think, admirable."

That Branwell was a clever lad, sometimes even quite brilliant, cannot be denied. That he was a "jack of all trades, and master of none" is, perhaps, a more accurate description of him.

☆ ☆ ☆ ☆

In September 1832 Charlotte paid a visit to Ellen Nussey's home, The Rydings at Birstall, and, like her brother who escorted her there, she would appear to have been much struck with the old turreted house in its sylvan setting of green lawns and chestnut trees. Branwell called it "Paradise" but Charlotte refrains from being too ecstatic about it. On the other hand, when Ellen repaid the visit (about a year later) she seems to have been much more impressed with the Parsonage House, expatiating later in life about the innate 'refinement' of the dove-coloured (not papered) walls, the sand-stoned (uncarpeted) floors, the spotless cleanliness everywhere. Branwell she sees as "a handsome boy, with 'tawny' hair; Emily, as "a tall, long-armed girl . . . extremely reserved in manner; Anne, as "shy". The difference (as Mrs Gaskell described it) was that "shyness would please, if it knew how; whereas, reserve is indifferent whether it pleases or not."

What particularly struck Ellen was the number of domestic animals that formed so much a part of the parsonage household. Dogs (like Emily's bull-mastiff, "Keeper", and Anne's spaniel "Flossy"); the cats ("Snowflake" and "Tom"); the canary ("Dick") and "Hero" (the hawk). Any stray or wounded creature in the neighbourhood found its way automatically to the Brontes' back door.

As to her reception by the family, Charlotte wrote later to say that "Papa and aunt are continually adducing you as an example for me to shape my actions and behaviour by. Emily and Anne say 'they never saw anyone they liked so well . . !'"

Most striking, perhaps, was Tabby's reaction. Charlotte describes her as "absolutely fascinated . . . (she) talks a great deal more nonsense about your ladyship than I care to repeat." This was the ultimate accolade, than which none could have been more sincere.

☆   ☆ ☆   ☆

A happy, happy time indeed and not fated to last or to be repeated in quite the same way. In the summer of 1835 (so often change for the Brontes came with the summer) Charlotte informed Ellen that "We are all about to divide, break up, separate. Emily is going to school, Branwell is going to London, and I am going to be a governess." It was the beginning of the long, hard road they were all thenceforth fated to tread. Things would never be seen in such unclouded sunlight again. Thereafter there was always a little too much shade.

With thoughts of that kind in mind I recall walking down Main Street a year or two ago with the intention of picking up the Keighley bus at the foot of the hill. Coming up was a young girl. She was wearing an ankle-length frock but swinging her hips none the less easily and gracefully for that. Her long hair was blown by the evening wind and her eyes were stone-set towards the moors. For one thrilling moment I had the impression I had come face to face with Emily herself. It was worth all the small treasures in the museum.

☆   ☆ ☆   ☆

Chapter 16

INTERLUDE – ROE HEAD (1835)

CHARLOTTE returned to Roe Head and Miss Wooler on 29th July 1835. This time she was accompanied by her sister Emily. The positions they were to occupy there were, respectively, teacher and pupil.

From Mr Bronte's point of view the arrangement must have appeared admirable. The cost of Emily's board and tuition would be defrayed by Charlotte from her small salary. In a manner of speaking Mr Bronte would be killing two birds with one stone.

As it transpired, in less than three months Emily was back home again at Haworth. So far as she was concerned that particular well-placed stone proved to be near-lethal in its effect.

"Liberty was the breath of Emily's nostrils;" wrote Charlotte (in her memoir to the 1850 edition of the poems of 'Ellis Bell') "without it she perished. The change from her own home to a school, and from her own very noiseless, very secluded, but unrestricted and unartificial mode of life, to one of disciplined routine (though under the kindest auspices) was what she failed in enduring . . . Every morning when she woke, the vision of home and the moors rushed on her, and darkened and saddened the day that lay before her. Nobody knew what ailed her but me. I knew only too well. In this struggle her health was quickly broken: her white face, attenuated form, and failing strength, threatened rapid decline. I felt in my heart she would die, if she did not go home, and with this conviction obtained her recall."

It may have been (if only sub-consciously) that Emily was still suffering from the after effects of her experience at Cowan Bridge and the early death of her sisters Maria and Elizabeth. Young as she then was her mind may well have registered that experience as light is absorbed by a photographic plate. But that she was 'a loner' in every sense of the word in undoubtedly the reason why she consistently failed to behave as one of a group anywhere outside her close family circle, and even there she went her own way in most things. The fact that she was most drawn to her sister Anne (and that mainly through their collaboration in the Gondal saga) was a saving factor, of course. There were times, too, when she most certainly had both feet firmly planted on the ground. This was proved by the obvious delight she took in the daily routine of household chores at the Parsonage, cooking and ironing and exchanging occasional crosstalk with Tabitha Aykroyd. But for most of the time she lived in a secret world of her own and it was one which none of the family was ever able to penetrate.

One cannot help suspecting also that she inclined to resent the minor role she was forced to assume at Roe Head in relation to that naturally assumed by her elder sister, to say nothing of the feeling of dependancy it must have imposed upon her. Contact with Charlotte could be very abrasive at times, as was to be proved on more than one occasion in later life and never more than when she had to act as mediator between mistress and pupil.

Mr Bronte himself must have been quite shaken by the turn of events and what he could not fail to regard as Emily's failure to co-operate with his plans for her settled future. So far as he could see there was no other course open than that each of his daughters should be trained to take up the position of governess in some (it was to be hoped) agreeable household. Where his son was concerned there appeared to be no problem whatever. It was confidently expected that a brilliant future awaited him somewhere in the world and the whole family subscribed to that belief. By the same token Mr Bronte deplored that anything or anyone should run counter to it.

He consoled himself with the reflection that for the time being, at any rate, one or other of his daughters might reasonably be employed at the beck and call of his sister-in-law and their servant 'Tabby'. It was as much as they could do to cope sometimes with the many and varied duties of the Parsonage and there were occasions when the domestic machinery ran anything but smooth and without friction. In the capacity of unpaid extra help (a saving grace) it mattered very little which of the girls was employed in that capacity. One need make no distinction between Emily and Anne. One might do as well as the other.

With no option, therefore, Anne was duly despatched to take her sister's place at Roe Head and Emily relieved her in the role of chore-master and general factotum at Haworth.

☆   ☆ ☆   ☆

Gentle, kind, long-suffering Anne . . . Of all the Bronte children, she it was who most resolutely set her nose to the grindstone and persevered in all that was demanded of her. Most likely she took after her father in this respect than whom none was more dogged in the cause of duty. Like him, too, she recognised her limitations and set her sights well within reach of them; something which could not be said for either Charlotte or Emily. Certainly not for her brother, Branwell.

Her resolution in this instance, however, was a little premature. She was only 16 when she took Emily's place at Roe Head and Charlotte was nearly four years her senior. The natural ascendancy of an older sister over a younger was aggravated (as in the case of Emily) by their relative positions in Miss Wooler's establishment. Charlotte, too, in continuing to maintain both of them found she was quite literally working for nothing at all and for no foreseeable end. Nor can it be said that she derived any real pleasure from what she was doing. She never much cared for children, anyway, and she was only too well aware of their increasing interference with the business of writing, which, though she would have been the last to admit it, was still (and always) the mainspring of all her actions. Being parted from Branwell and active participation in the everyday story of Angrian folk was bad enough. It was even worse that she found herself unable to confide in Anne to the extent that had been possible with Emily. As a consequence she became more desperately unhappy than she ever remembered to have been since leaving Cowan Bridge.

She had another and more immediate cause for concern. Until the end of the year 1835 the one bright star, the very light of her life, had been Branwell. On him she had focussed all her wavering intentions. Everything was to be endured so long as he should prosper and make it possible for them all to share in his prosperity. It was at this point in time and just when they needed most that he should do well that Branwell failed them all, completely.

☆   ☆ ☆   ☆

Chapter 17

INTERLUDE – LONDON (Autumn 1835)

"BRANWELL IS going to London" wrote Charlotte in that same letter to Ellen Nussey in which she announced her return to Roe Head. The move on her part was necessary on account of the fact that "papa would have enough to do with his limited income should Branwell be placed at the Royal Academy."

With this object in view her brother (so far as we know) took the Keighley coach to Charing Cross some time in the autumn of 1835. The actual date is not known because no member of the Bronte family ever mentioned it. Nor did Mrs Gaskell, who would appear to have us believe that he never made the journey at all.

We have no reason to doubt that he did. Branwell himself wrote a fictional account of his visit to London (in the "Adventures of Charles Wentworth"). He also mentioned it later to some of his Bradford friends, including the sculptor, Leyland.

One can assume therefore that some little time after Charlotte and Emily departed for Roe Head, Branwell left for London, liberally supplied with money by his father and some of his father's old Thornton friends together with letters of introduction (from William Robinson and other local artists) to facilitate his entry to the Royal Academy Schools (then located in Somerset House). It is also safe to assume that none of these introductory letters were ever presented in the right quarters.

As far as we can ascertain, Branwell put up at the Chapter Coffee House, opposite Ivy Lane in Paternoster Row. This former haunt of authors, booksellers, and clerical gentlemen could justly claim later to have provided accommodation for all the Bronte family at some time or other. Mr Bronte stayed there when negotiating for his first appointment at Wethersfield; Charlotte, Emily and Anne (as will be seen) all availed themselves of the respectable protection it had to offer.

It lay in the shade of St. Paul's, at the very heart of the publishing and bookselling business (the whole area of which was heavily blitzed during the War). All that now remains is a narrow passage hemmed in on both sides by modern office blocks. A depressing place and one entirely without soul.

"I am quite familiar at the Chapter Coffee House and know all the geniuses there," boasted Thomas Chatterton in 1770 (writing to his mother in Bristol). He was 17 at the time (only a year younger than Branwell) and far from being as successful as he made out was actually starving in a Holborn garret. A short time later he poisoned himself. Poor Branwell was not to find so easy a way out. His means to that end was a much slower and more painful progress.

☆   ☆ ☆   ☆

What he similarly had to face up to was his own inadequacy. When confronted in the London art galleries by the work of men like Gainsborough and Reynolds he was only too conscious of his lack of any real talent. Nor had he the will-power to apply himself to his chosen trade. By dint of such application he may reasonably have earned some sort of a living as an honest journeyman artist (as failed writers often make good journalists). He preferred to drift as the fancy took him, and that was nowhere in particular.

He drifted about London in the same desultory fashion, more and more intimidated by the magnificence of the great city and growing more and more bitter with the realisation that it appeared to want nothing that he had to offer. A pathetic and unprepossessing figure he must have seemed, small in stature, with 'carroty' hair and dressed (like all the Bronte children) in outmoded clothes. It must have been with unimaginable relief that he lighted at last on the Castle Tavern in High Holborn.

Branwell was always at his best and brightest in convivial

company and what better place to find it than in a pub? He had proved that in Haworth and this particular tavern had a reputation that extended even as far as the Black Bull and the White Lion. The boxing fraternity there were always talking about Tom Spring, pugilist extraordinary and one-time champion of England. And here he was, presiding over the assembled company as mine host (literally king) of the notorious Castle . . .

In no time at all Branwell was holding his own with the best of them, both as regards his capacity for drinking and for his even more remarkable gift of the gab. Nobody questioned his ability in that direction. There was no need to apologise here for his short-comings and consequently no further need to abase himself in the presence of more exalted company. Branwell was at home again, which was anywhere he knew he was most welcome.

The Castle Tavern was situated almost opposite the Holborn end of Chancery Lane on that same road that once saw the tumbrils rumbling from Newgate Prison to Tyburn Tree and the holiday-making at public executions. Fielding's Tom Jones entered London this way and put up at the neighbouring Bull & Gate. Not a stone's throw away, in Kingsgate Street, Red Lion Square, lodged the immortal Sarah Gamp with her addiction to the same occasional glass from a bottle.

All this would have meant little to Branwell Bronte, no doubt, but I can't help wondering if a trip down nearby Brooke Street ever dampened his artificially high spirits. In a garret at No. 39 (at the house of "Mrs Angell, the sail-maker") that other "marvellous boy" took a far more potent draught than any that ever passed his lips. The house was still standing then (not having been destroyed till 1880).

☆   ☆ ☆   ☆

As far as we know, Branwell stayed no longer than a week in London before his money and his credit ran out at Tom Spring's Castle Tavern. Presumably he held a return ticket on the coach to Haworth or may have budgeted sufficient to defray the cost of the homeward journey. The fact remains that, like the prodigal son or the proverbial bad penny, he landed at last on the Parsonage doorstep.

His ingenuity at spinning yarns must have been taxed quite considerably on that particular trip. But did Mr Bronte, Aunt Branwell, and his sister Emily really accept that he had been robbed of all his money on the journey out? And if they were prepared to believe such a cock-and-bull story on what did they presume he had been living for the past few days? Charlotte was at Roe Head (with Anne) which was probably just as well. One can imagine what her reactions would have been. What they were later must have sunk Branwell in her estimation for good and all.

The one thing Branwell had not been robbed of, however, was his self-confidence. He may have felt (though only temporarily) that he was not fated to compete on an equal footing with even the Willaim Robinsons of this world. No matter. When one door closed for him, another was bound to open somewhere. A writer of his calibre must succeed where a third rate painter had no chance whatever. By the end of the year he was writing to the editor of Blackwood's Magazine in Edinburgh to the effect that refusal to accept what he had to offer in that direction would be a loss which they could not afford to ignore.

They chose to ignore him on three separate occasions and each time Branwell became more hysterically insistent on his claims to their attention. Had he been anywhere near as obstinate with the authorities at the Royal Academy Schools he might well have reaped some reward from his efforts. As it was he found himself defeated on both counts and through no other reason than a failure to please anyone but himself and his own insufferable ego.

☆   ☆ ☆   ☆

Chapter 18

INTERLUDE – LAW HILL, SOUTHOWRAM, HALIFAX
(? Autumn 1837 - ? December 1838)

SOMETIME IN 1837 (probably in the autumn of that year) Emily Bronte left Haworth to take a position as teacher at Law Hill, a girls' school (of some 20 pupils) run by Miss Elizabeth Patchett at Southowram, a suburb of Halifax.

"I have had one letter from her since her departure," wrote Charlotte to Ellen Nussey in October 1837. "It gives an appalling account of her duties: hard labour from six in the morning until near eleven at night, with only one half-hour of exercise between. This is slavery. I fear she will never stand it."

Mrs Gaskell's only reference to this episode in Emily's life is the above quotation from Charlotte's letter and a later remark to the effect that "Emily had given up her situation in the Halifax school, at the expiration of six months of arduous trial, on account of her health, which could only be re-established by the bracing moorland air and free life of home."

Recent research, however, would appear to have proved that Emily's stay at Law Hill extended over a period of 18 months. One piece of evidence produced to substantiate this is the poem beginning "A little while, a little while/The noisy crowd are barred away" (dated December 1838) and presumably written from the point of view of a teacher with regard to her pupils. Charlotte (for some reason or another) amended this poem in the 1850 edition of her sisters' works, giving an entirely opposite impression and suggesting that it might well have been composed during Emily's short stay at Roe Head.

There is added evidence in the fact that Mrs Gaskell makes no mention of Emily's whereabouts during this

18-month period (apart from being at home during what are obviously end-of-term holidays). One is tempted to regard the discrete silence on this point in the same light as the reticence maintained (both by the Bronte family and Mrs Gaskell) with regard to Branwell's parallel trip to London in 1835. What is to be deduced therefrom can only be matter for speculation.

☆   ☆ ☆   ☆

I was led to reflect a great deal more on this problem when it befell me to make closer acquaintance with the immediate neighbourhood. One summer evening I took the road out of Halifax that climbs all the way to Southowram and Beacon Hill (where the school was situated). I walked, on account of having just missed the bus and another not being due for at least another half-hour.

Halifax is bracketed with Hell and Hull as being a place from which the Good Lord is proverbially invoked to deliver us. Certainly, gazed down on from the hills that surround it, smoke seems to rise everywhere from countless chimneys as though from the depths of the nether regions. The carpet-works here, they say, are the biggest in the world — and I can well believe it. An industrial complex of that kind can hardly be expected not to leave its mark on the landscape, though not necessarily an altogether black one. I can't speak for Hell or Hull but I found Halifax most attractive at close quarters. Its streets are spacious and glittering and it has some of the finest modern buildings I have yet seen. For sheer breath-taking magnificence there is nothing to beat the new headquarters of the world-famous Halifax Building Society.

From Southowram (rather sleepy and old-fashioned by comparison) one gets the surrounding country into some sort of perspective and the panoramic view of moor and farmland is conceivably much as Emily might have remembered it. Law Hill is a group of 18th-Century buildings enclosing an inner courtyard. It struck me as being poised on the edge of the world, overlooking outer space like some coastguard station on a bluff headland. I met few people in the neighbourhood and none I judged to be inclined to conversation. They seemed to sense I was a stranger there and to be avoided as one who might ask awkward questions they had no wish to answer. I couldn't help wondering what their reactions might be to anything involving them with the Brontes. Did they know that Emily had once been here? And if they knew, did they really care?

Emily herself, as much a stranger in these parts as anywhere else on earth, must often have come up against this failure to communicate what she was thinking or feeling. For instance, a former pupil at Law Hill reports her as having once informed her small charges that she thought more of the house-dog than she did of them. Charlotte could not have been crueller and certainly never gave vent to her suppressed emotions quite so outrageously. It is obvious that Emily was anything but happy in her work. As to her suitability, it is matter for wonder that Miss Patchett could have put up with her for six months, let alone eighteen.

In any case, how could Emily herself have endured it? Charlotte, much more determined to persevere with an ill-chosen career, stayed less than three months in her first post as a governess and under a year in her second attempt to come to terms with uncongenial employers. Is it conceivable that her sister could have been so much more patient and forgiving without there being some compensatory reason for not flying back home as she did from Roe Head?

We know that she wrote some of her more mature poems at Law Hill, that she visited neighbouring Shibden Hall and High Sunderland and drew to a certain extent on her impressions of these country mansions when called on later to provide a setting for the Lintons at Thrushcross Grange and the Earnshaws at Wuthering Heights. How she found the necessary time for such pleasurable pursuits is a mystery, however, when one takes into account Charlotte's statement that her "hard labour" there extended "from six in the morning until near eleven at night, with only one half-hour of exercise between."

As far as we know, Emily was never in love with anyone. But that is only as far as we know. Is it possible that an affair of some kind detained her at Law Hill? From whence did she draw the inspiration for Heathcliff's almost diabolical passion for Catherine Earnshaw? Is it too much to suggest that it may have originated in some purely personal experience?

Speculation, of course. But it may well account for what must otherwise remain completely unaccountable.

☆   ☆ ☆   ☆

Chapter 19

INTERLUDE – ROE HEAD (continued)
(January 1836 - May 1838)

AFTER BRANWELL'S abortive attempt to make a career for himself in London Charlotte in her turn became more and more disillusioned with her own prospects at Roe Head. Unlike her brother, however, she was not able to dismiss her own failings quite so lightly. Charlotte, indeed, made hard work of whatever came her way.

"If you knew my thoughts;" (she wrote to Ellen Nussey, in May 1836) "the dreams that absorb me; and the fiery imagination that at times eats me up and makes me feel society, as it is, wretchedly insipid, you would pity and I dare say despise me."

The society she found so "wretchedly insipid" was what she was forced to put up with as a teacher in the shape of those "fat-headed oafs" (her own words) who were continually interrupting her day-dreams with lessons to be corrected. "I have some qualities" (she said) "that make me very miserable, some feelings that you can have no participation in – that few, very few, people in the world can at all understand. I strive to conceal and suppress them as much as I can; but they burst out sometimes, and then those who see the explosion despise me, and I hate myself for days afterwards . . . "

Mary Taylor (the more intelligent of her two correspondents) would have appreciated what lay behind such a confession, but Ellen Nussey must have been sorely puzzled, maybe a little embarrassed by that kind of soul-searching. She put it all down to the fact that Charlotte was working too hard, and indeed she was. But that she was working against the grain of her own nature was something Ellen could truly "have no participation in." Charlotte had never seen fit to confide in her where her real inclinations lay.

In consequence the more Ellen counselled her to put her trust in the will of God the more guilty Charlotte felt herself to be in failing to measure up to such high moral standards. "If the Doctrine of Calvin be true" (she wrote) "I am already an outcast." It was religious melancholia with a vengeance and how she managed to survive it without a complete nervous breakdown says much for Charlotte's powers of endurance.

Occasional visits to both her school-friends (they lived within easy reach of Roe Head) helped to lighten her spirits a little, but what cheered her most was being home for the Christmas holidays of 1836/37 and the determination she formed there to do something towards advancing her writing career, so long neglected for mundane affairs. Following Branwell's efforts to engage the attention of Blackwood's Magazine, Charlotte in her turn unburdened her heart to Robert Southey, the Poet Laureate. She was luckier than her brother for Southey took pains to answer her letter though it was a couple of months before he got round to it.

His reply was kind and courteous but it inclined to the opinion that she had time on her hands which might be put to better use. "The day-dreams in which you habitually indulge" (he wrote) "are likely to induce a distempered state of mind and in proportion as all the ordinary uses of the world seem to you flat and unprofitable, you will be unfitted for them without becoming fitted for anything else. Literature cannot be the business of a woman's life, and it ought not to be. The more she is engaged in her proper duties, the less leisure will she have for it, even as an accomplishment and a recreation . . ."

How well he diagnosed the situation which Charlotte then found herself to be in and how little he understood what motivated her desire to change it. Nevertheless, he was sufficiently appreciative of what she must have sent him (her letter and its contents have never come to light) to give her, at least, a little encouragement. "Write poetry for its own sake"; (he counselled) "not in a spirit of emulation, and not with a view to celebrity; the less you aim at that the more likely you will be to deserve and finally to obtain it."

Charlotte was not slow in writing back and putting Southey wise to the fact that she was anything but a dilettante but one who had necessarily to work hard for the barest of livings. Southey was intrigued enough to suggest she might visit him if and when she happened to be in the neighbourhood of Keswick, where he was then living. Poor Charlotte . . . It was as much as she could do to scrape together enough money to transport her the twenty odd miles between Roe Head and Haworth.

Southey died in 1843. One can't help regretting that he missed (by a mere four years) the furore that followed the publication of Jane Eyre. As it turned out eventually the business of one woman's life was more than justified.

☆   ☆ ☆   ☆

During the summer holidays of 1837 Miss Wooler (for family reasons) moved her school from Roe Head, Mirfield to Heald's House on Dewsbury Moor (not far from where Mr Bronte took up his first appointment in Yorkshire). Charlotte described the atmosphere there as "poisonous" but it was not only the climatic conditions she had in mind. She was becoming more and more desperate with regard to the position she occupied in the establishment and the increasing responsibility thrust upon her owing to Miss Wooler's frequent absence. Southey was right when he referred to her "day-dreams" as "likely to induce a distempered state of mind." Certainly "all the ordinary uses of the world" never seemed more "flat and unprofitable" than at that time, in that place.

To make matters worse, Anne took suddenly ill just before Christmas that year. Mrs Gaskell describes her symptoms as "a slight cough, a pain at her side, a difficulty of breathing." Charlotte's mind flew immediately to the "consumption" which had carried off her sisters Maria and Elizabeth and she was quick to reveal her suspicions to Miss Wooler. That good lady, irritated no doubt by Charlotte's inclination to make mountains out of molehills, was of the opinion that Anne was suffering from nothing more than the effects of a bad cold.

This was too much for Charlotte. Those feelings she described to Ellen as "striving to conceal and suppress" burst out again and she quarrelled most bitterly with her employer. Poor Miss Wooler was reduced to tears and then to writing to Mr Brontë about it. He could do no more than remove Anne from the school. She was not to return there after the Christmas holidays.

The wonder is that Charlotte did. Her powers of endurance were really quite remarkable and one can't help feeling that she was inclined to underplay her capabilities in that direction. At the same time she may have been influenced by Miss Wooler's desire to let bygones be bygones and a sense of her own guilt in having reacted rather unjustly. Nevertheless she afterwards admitted that she would have felt a great deal better about her employer "if she had turned me out of doors . . ."

It says much for the basic good nature of both of them that they were able to come to an amicable agreement, but it was another thing altogether to make it work. Charlotte's own health very soon broke down under the renewed strain and this time she was forced to seek medical advice rather than rely on Ellen Nussey's doubtful consolation. If she was not to break down completely it was essential that she should leave Dewsbury Moor . . .

In deference to that advice (and perhaps with no sense of having betrayed her trust) Charlotte rejoined her sister at Haworth on the 23rd of May, 1838. She had learned a lot about the difficult business of getting on with other people. She still had a great deal more to learn.

☆   ☆ ☆   ☆

Chapter 20

HAWORTH — (May 1838 - April 1839)

FOR ALMOST A year the three sisters were together again where they most loved to be, under the protective roof of the Parsonage House at Haworth.

If Mr Bronte continued to absent himself from their company and Aunt Branwell occasionally appeared as disagreeable as ever, it was no great matter. As Catullus truly said, "What is more blessed than to throw cares aside, as the mind puts down its burden and, weary with the labour of far journeys, we return home and rest on the couch we longed for? This alone is worth all that labour." It was a sentiment both Charlotte and Emily most heartily subscribed to. Anne (whose experience of exile had so far been brief) would not be long in taking it for granted.

Branwell, of course, was at home nowhere but in convivial company. He had resumed painting, a small studio having been found for him (off Manningham Lane, in Bradford). He even succeeded in obtaining a few small commissions from local worthies who were pleased enough to sit for their portraits without demanding to be immortalised in the process. But the project never really got off the ground, except as a flight of fancy. One suspects that Branwell was most happy in the company of would-be artists like himself when they were not working. In particular he cultivated the friendship of Joseph Leyland (the Halifax sculptor) who at least had something to show for his apprenticeship.

More often than not he was at home with his sisters at weekends and we have one delightful picture of them all happy together on such an occasion, just after Charlotte's return from Roe Head (or rather, Dewsbury Moor). Mr Bronte had suggested that maybe the company of her old school-friends, Mary and Martha Taylor, might help to restore her good humour, and for once in a way he managed to prescribe exactly the right treatment. To Ellen Nussey, in June 1838, she writes (with an enthusiasm sadly lacking in previous correspondence) — "They are making such a noise about me I cannot write any more. Mary is playing on the piano; Martha is chattering as fast as her little tongue can run; and Branwell is standing before her, laughing at her vivacity . . . "

This may well have been the normal thing in a normal household of that time, but in the Bronte home it was something quite extraordinary. Such gay abandon, such a flinging of bonnets in the air, must have seemed (to Charlotte, anyway) like tempting Providence to do its worst. Providence, of course, was never backward in obliging.

From the back windows of the Parsonage, even on a June day such as this, grey clouds, tending to become blacker, were often to be seen by those most alive to such portents. The Brontes were able to spot them long before they loomed large enough to threaten the coming storm. It was part of their nature.

☆   ☆ ☆   ☆

Mr Bronte himself may well have had some reservations with regard to this outburst of high spirits. Time for him was normally measured by the slow ticking of the clock on the stairs, regularly wound at nine every night. That Aunt Branwell joined in the fun is even less likely. She was more apt than anyone to escape from too cheerful company to the peace and quiet of her own bedroom. It reminded her too forcibly of what she had lost in the way of friendly society by putting duty at Haworth before pleasure in Penzance. No doubt she endured her splendid isolation the more obstinately on that account.

It is possible too that she had not yet given up brooding over what had happened during the Christmas holidays when her obstinacy had been opposed by something even more obdurate. Tabitha Aykroyd, the parsonage servant, whilst on an errand in Haworth's main street, had slipped on the ice and fractured her leg. "She was past the age for any very active service, being nearer seventy than sixty at the time of the accident," wrote Mrs Gaskell. Aunt Branwell regarded the occasion as a heaven-sent opportunity for getting rid of her.

'Tabby' had a sister living in the village with whom she might conveniently be boarded out. She would not lack for any social service the Parsonage was still able to provide. So Aunt Branwell argued and Mr Bronte was eventually won round to agree to. The girls took a different view, however. Tabby was "one of the family" so far as they were concerned and was to be treated as such. If not, the elders would have only themselves to blame for what might follow.

What followed was dire in the extreme. The girls went on 'hunger strike.' "At tea-time, they were sad and silent," Mrs Gaskell reported, "and the meal went away untouched by any of the three. So it was at breakfast; they did not waste many words on the subject, but each word they did utter was weighty." Finally, "the resolution was rescinded, and Tabby was allowed to remain a helpless invalid entirely dependent upon them."

Aunt Branwell bowed out as gracefully as she could in the circumstances but she must have been considerably shaken. That they were fast growing beyond her control was pretty obvious. It was even more so now when she heard their voices raised in song and uninhibited laughter.

☆   ☆ ☆   ☆

That scene round the parlour piano in June 1838 might have come straight out of one of Jane Austen's novels with the difference that it entailed nothing in the way of matchmaking. To be sure it was hinted (by Charlotte) that Mary Taylor was disposed to be a little sweet on Branwell. Branwell, however, was decidedly cool in that direction.

It seems quite remarkable that none of the girls would appear to have considered matrimony as a solution to their economic problems. Charlotte, Emily, and Anne . . . respectively 22, 20, and 18 at the time . . . might naturally be expected to have contemplated such a possibility. Yet, like their brother, they seem (most unnaturally) to have gone out of their way not to encourage overtures of that kind.

Charlotte, in fact, did receive a proposal of marriage in March 1839 — from no less a person than Ellen's brother, the Rev. Henry Nussey — but she turned him down flat. She was kindly disposed towards him as an amiable man (she told Ellen) but "she had not, could not have, that intense attachment which would make me willing to die for him . . ." Mrs Gaskell says "Matrimony did not enter into the scheme of her life, but good, sound, earnest labour did." One might be forgiven for refusing to believe it. She did marry, in her own sweet time, as we all know, but the brother of her best friend was anything but the right choice for her (even though it might well have proved a marriage of particular convenience). Henry Nussey was far too cold and calculating for Charlotte's taste. We know now that he was listing and ticking off such proposals as they failed to materialise.

What Charlotte demanded was a Grand Passion, one that would literally sweep her off her feet. It was evidenced in her own words to Ellen . . . "if he were a clever man, and loved me, the whole world, weighed in the balance against his smallest wish, should be light as air."

There was never anyone quite like that in Charlotte's restricted circle of friends. There was never anyone quite like that anywhere . . . Mr Rochester was, perhaps, the nearest approach to such an ideal. But he, after all, was only a figment of the imagination.

☆   ☆ ☆   ☆

Chapter 21

INTERLUDE – BLAKE HALL, MIRFIELD
(April 1839 - December 1839)

THE SAME DAY I first went to Roe Head I spent over an hour looking round Mirfield for Blake Hall. "Never heard of it," was the general response to my enquiries. One old chap grew quite indignant when I ventured the opinion that he must have done. "Been here, off and on, most of my life," he said. "If anyone should know, I should."

It was in the bar of the Three Nuns that a young man (obviously a student on vacation) told me the house was pulled down in 1954. He was not a student of the Brontes. In fact he was doing a thesis on the Luddites and, as he said, this was one of the areas most associated with them.

His parting comment was rather an illuminating one. "I don't think it's because they don't know," he said, (meaning about the destruction of Blake Hall). "I think it's because they don't want to know. They don't seem to want to know about anything."

Like myself, he was all too obviously a stranger in the neighbourhood.

☆   ☆ ☆   ☆

Anne Bronte would have shed no tears over the loss of Blake Hall. She went there as a governess in April 1839 and returned to Haworth (on dismissal from her post) in December of the same year. By all accounts she had a pretty ghastly time.

"I can conceive few situations more harassing than that wherein, however you may long for success, however you may labour to fulfil your duty, your efforts are baffled and set at naught by those beneath you, and unjustly censured and misjudged by those above," she wrote, in

Chapter IV of her novel "Agnes Grey."

She was writing about the Bloomfields of Wellwood. What she had in mind was the Inghams of Blake Hall, Mirfield.

In a letter to Ellen Nussey on April 15th Charlotte announced her sister's departure in the following rather deprecatory terms: "Poor child! . . . she left us last Monday; no one went with her; it was her own wish that she might be allowed to go alone, as she thought she could manage better, and summon more courage, if thrown entirely upon her own resources . . . I hope she'll do. You would be astonished what a sensible, clever letter she writes; it is only the talking part that I fear. But I do seriously apprehend that Mrs - - - will sometimes conclude that she had a natural impediment in her speech . . ."

There is, surely, a sly dig at her elder sister's condescending attitude towards her in Anne's interchange of dialogue between Agnes Grey and her sister Mary:

Mary: "Help me you cannot, Agnes; and I cannot go out with *you* – I have far too much to do."

Agnes: "Then let me help you."

Mary: "You cannot, indeed, dear child. Go and practise your music, or play with the kitten."

It is there too in Mrs Grey's reception of her daughter's proposal that she might amend the family's worsening situation by going out to work as a governess – "But, my love, you have not learned to take care of *yourself* yet: and young children require more judgement and experience to manage than elder ones."

One can't help feeling that Anne had Aunt Branwell in mind here. It is the sort of comment one might expect from her.

The fact remains that Anne was determined to pull her weight and the more so for being continually treated like a child. That she was the youngest in the family should and would not be held against her in the matter of capability. Her elders had so far all failed in that direction; Charlotte, at Roe Head; Emily, at Law Hill; Branwell, in London. It would be a smack in the eye for the lot of them if she could succeed in keeping her place and making a success of her situation at Blake Hall.

Poor child, indeed ... Charlotte was not far off the mark, really, for all her condescension. That Anne, in stiffening up her resolution, was still necessarily having to fight back the tears is plainly evidenced in the description of Agnes Grey's thoughts in the gig taking her from home to her first situation at Wellwood: "We crossed the valley, and began to ascend the opposite hill. As we were toiling up, I looked back again: there was the village spire, and the old grey parsonage beyond it, basking in a slanting beam of sunshine — it was but a sickly ray, but the village and surrounding hills were all in sombre shade . . ."

If the Inghams of Blake Hall were anything like the Bloomfields of Wellwood then this last look back was indeed a portent of things to come. In both cases governess Anne and governess Agnes were responsible only for the two older children of their respective employers but if Tom Bloomfield (age 7) and his sister Mary Ann (age 6) were anything to go by they were something much more than a handful. They were devils incarnate.

Tom's pet hobby was trapping wild birds with sticks and cords. "Sometimes I give them to the cat;" he said, "sometimes I cut them in pieces with my penknife; but the next, I mean to roast alive."

Mary Ann (as befitting the gentler sex) showed off her own particular brand of ill-humour by rolling on the floor, screaming, and resolutely refusing to repeat her lessons. Agnes Grey was reduced to either forcibly holding both of them down or blocking them off in a corner with a chair past which there was no escape till their set task was done.

"I found they had no notion of going with *me*:" (says the fictional governess) "I must go with *them* wherever they chose to lead me. I must run, walk, or stand, exactly as it suited their fancy." In consequence she was frequently told off by Mr Bloomfield for their dirty and untidy appearance whilst Mrs Bloomfield merely wrung her hands in exasperation over what she considered was a stupid inability on the part of the governess to cope with the natural high spirits of her darling children.

Anne Bronte (unlike her sister Charlotte) was never one

to exaggerate her problems and difficulties. The vividness with which she describes the experiences of Agnes Grey (in what is pre-eminently a plain, unvarished tale) seems much nearer truth than fiction. One is forced to think so, anyway.

The famous episode of the handful of nestling birds, for instance, which Master Tom intended torturing so cruelly and on which (to put them out of their misery) Agnes Grey dropped a large, flat stone . . . Surely it was not in gentle Anne's nature to portray events so outrageous if they had no foundation in fact? On the other hand it shows a determination on her part which she was far from being credited with by her family. A wry sense of humour too . . . For instance, when Mrs Bloomfield (defending her son's treatment of dumb animals) observes, "You seem to have forgotten that the creatures were all created for our convenience" Agnes comments, most pithily, "I thought that doctrine admitted some doubt."

Whatever there may be of truth in the fiction of Agnes Grey, one thing its author and her heroine have in common: they were both dismissed for supposed incompetency. "Mrs Bloomfield sent for me," says Agnes, "and soberly told me that after Midsummer my services would be no longer required . . . my character and general conduct were unexceptional; but the children had made so little improvement since my arrival, that Mr Bloomfield and she felt it their duty to seek some other mode of instruction."

It was a cool appraisal of Anne's own situation, or lack of it, with the Inghams of Blake Hall. Returning home at the end of that year, she had to admit she had failed in her endeavours. But at least she could boast that it had not been for want of trying. As for her young charges having to seek "some other mode of instruction . . ." We should have been tempted, today, to suggest Borstal or a similar form of approved schooling for possible corrective treatment.

☆   ☆ ☆   ☆

Chapter 22

INTERLUDE – STONEGAPPE, LOTHERSDALE, Nr SKIPTON (May 1839 - July 1839)

IN HER LETTER of April 15th 1839 to Ellen Nussey announcing Anne's engagement as governess to the Inghams of Blake Hall Charlotte referred humourously to the fact that she had discovered in herself "a talent for cleaning, sweeping up hearths, dusting rooms, making beds, etc." so if everything else failed she could turn her hand to that. "I won't be a cook"; (she said) "I hate cooking. I won't be a nursery-maid, nor a lady's maid, far less a lady's companion, or a mantua-maker, or a straw-bonnet maker, or a taker-in of plain work. I won't be anything but a housemaid . . ."

A few weeks later she took up the position of nursery-governess to the family of Mr & Mrs Sidgwick at Stone-gappe, a large mansion in the region of Lothersdale, a village some four miles from Skipton in North Yorkshire.

She would have done better to stick to her original intention, in spite of having obviously made it with her tongue in her cheek. She could not have fared worse unless she had decided on exhanging duties with Anne and the Inghams at Blake Hall.

The Sidgwicks were a typical example of the wealthy manufacturing classes who, at the time of the Industrial Revolution, were fast taking over from the landowners of Elizabethan times. Mr Sidgwick's father owned cotton mills in Skipton. Mrs Sidgwick was the daughter of a rich manufacturer who had extensive property in Keighley. They had four children of whom Charlotte had charge only of the two youngest, Mathilda (aged 6) and John (aged 4).

"More riotous, perverse, unmanageable cubs never grew." (wrote Charlotte, to her sister Emily, in June

1839). "As for correcting them, I soon quickly found that was entirely out of the question: they are to do as they like. A complaint to Mrs Sidgwick brings only black looks upon oneself, and unjust, partial excuses to screen the children ..." It would seem she was in the position of faring no better than Anne with the progeny of this 'nouveau riche' class of employer, "proud as peacocks and wealthy as Jews" as she described them to Emily.

It was a great pity in some respects for the scene which daily confronted the governess, looking out from her schoolroom window over the valley of the Lother, might well have been an inspiration to her from its indescribable loveliness. But, in the words of Bishop Heber's wellknown hymn, "Though every prospect pleases/And only man is vile" it was poor consolation to Charlotte that she was unable to enjoy it. "I said in my last letter" (she told Emily) "that Mrs Sidgwick did not know me. I now begin to find that she does not intend to know me, that she cares nothing in the world about me except to contrive how the greatest possible quantity of labour may be squeezed out of me, and to that end she overwhelms me with oceans of needlework, yards of cambric to hem, muslin nightcaps to make, and, above all things, dolls to dress."

The scorn in that last phrase about 'dolls' is almost searing and provides as good a clue to Charlotte's character as one is likely to find anywhere. It explains why she was never able to get on with children in that she found it impossible to penetrate their make-believe world of toys and games in spite of her ability to construct make-believe worlds of her own. She knew well enough how to work. She had never been taught how to play.

The same might be said of all the family, with the possible exception of Branwell who, like Peter Pan, never quite grew up. The loss of their mother when they were all so young made little adults of them from the start, and life with father and Aunt Branwell was no help. They at all times had to keep down any show of high-spiritedness and they were firm in restraining others for that very reason. It is no wonder that they failed in the day to day business of dealing with the children of their employers who had never known such restraint.

There was the occasion, for instance, when Charlotte was entrusted with the care of little John Sidgwick on his parents absence from home and instructed at all costs to keep him out of the stable-yard where he was likely to land up in a right old mess. Brother William (some five years older) preferred to differ in that respect and encouraged the boy to follow his example in defying authority even to the extent of stoning the governess when she attempted to entice him back into the house. One of these brickbats opened up a nasty cut on Charlotte's forehead but she preferred to make light of it when questioned next day by Mrs Sidgwick at the communal dining table. It was only "an accident" she said.

Nothing impressed her young charges more than her obvious unwillingness to tell tales out of school about them and from that time on she found she was able to manage them a great deal better. Indeed so much had young John taken this particular lesson to heart that a day or two later at the same dinner table he slipped his hand into Charlotte's and exclaimed, involuntarily, "I love 'ou, Miss Bronte." Such a display of unwarrantable affection was too much for Mrs Sidgwick, however. "Love the *governess*, my dear!" she expostulated. It was something she could not possibly bring herself to believe and was certainly not prepared to tolerate as between master and servant.

I can't help thinking that poor Charlotte might have got on a lot better with everybody, including her employers and her employers' children, if she had shown the same firmness of spirit that she allowed her heroine, Jane Eyre, to indulge in. It was this tendency to answer back and to give as good as she got that most endeared her to Mr Rochester than whom no one could have been more aristocratic and overbearing. But Charlotte was at her best when day-dreaming about life as it might be. She was increasingly unable to deal with life as it existed outside the realms of fiction.

That Mrs Sidgwick ought to have seen her as no mere servant but as one to be treated as equal, if not superior, to herself must have been Charlotte's constant cause for complaint. She was unable to give voice to it, however, except in the form of veiled criticism in her letters to Emily and Ellen and as final justification in Jane Eyre. Mrs Sidgwick means nothing to us and would have long gone to her grave unremarked and unknown but for the part she played in the continuing story of her unconsidered employee.

☆   ☆ ☆   ☆

John Greenwood, Mrs Sidgwick's father, owned a large house called Swarcliffe, near Harrogate, and there he liked to entertain his family during the summer months. In June 1839 Charlotte accompanied the Sidgwicks on one of their periodical visits there and was by no means enlivened by the change of air from that of Stonegappe. She wrote Ellen Nussey to the effect that "the house was full of company" and that she was given charge of "a set of pampered, spoilt, and turbulent children" whom she was "expected constantly to amuse as well as instruct . . ." In consequence her spirits (she said) were reduced "to the lowest state of exhaustion" and she was "taken to task on the subject by Mrs Sidgwick with a stress of manner and a harshness of language scarcely credible."

Poor Charlotte broke down and wept. "I thought I had done my best — strained every nerve to please her — and to be treated in that way merely because I was shy and sometimes melancholy was too bad." She was tempted to give up there and then but she managed to prolong the agony a little while longer. Patience, she thought, might still help her to come to terms with a mistress with whom she had never had five minutes conversation, apart from when she was being scolded.

Her resolution lasted no more than a couple of weeks. Writing to Ellen again on the 26th of July, this time from Haworth, she had to confess that she had "left Stonegappe a week since." She was never so glad, she said, to get out of a house in her life.

If she had any regrets at all it was on Mr Sidgwick's

account and no one elses. The one occasion she recalled with pleasure during her three months period of employment was when he "walked out with his children, and I had orders to follow a little behind. As he strolled on through his fields, with his magnificent Newfoundland dog at his side, he looked very like what a frank, wealthy, Conservative gentleman ought to be. He spoke freely and unaffectedly to the people he met, and though he indulged his children and allowed them to tease himself far too much, he would not suffer them grossly to insult others . . ."

Charlotte always got on better with men than she did with women. In her novels she was far more successful in portraying her heroes than her heroines, except in what she put in them of herself. And that was mostly wishful thinking.

☆   ☆ ☆   ☆

Chapter 23

HAWORTH (July 1839 - March 1841)

THOUGH CHARLOTTE was never happier than when at home she found, on her return from Stonegappe, that Mr Bronte and Aunt Branwell could be quite as frustrating as Mrs Sidgwick. It happened that Ellen Nussey proposed spending a few weeks by the sea (at Bridlington, on the East Yorkshire coast) and she invited Charlotte to accompany her. The elders of the Bronte family, however, were dead set against it.

The first spanner thrown in the works was the counter-proposal by papa and aunt that Charlotte should spend a fortnight's holiday with them in Liverpool. It was no more than "a sort of castle in the air" wrote Charlotte to Ellen on August 4th 1839. She doubted if it would ever assume a more solid shape. "Aunt – like many other elderly people – " (she said) "likes to talk of such things; but when it comes to putting them into actual execution, she rather falls off . . ."

Ten days later she is still harping on the same theme. No gig is available to take her from Haworth to Leeds for at least another fortnight, if then . . . "Papa decidedly objects to my going by the coach . . ." she says. "Aunt proclaims against the weather, and the roads, and the four winds of heaven . . ." It was quite obvious to her (no doubt to Ellen also) that every obstacle was being put in the way of the proposed trip.

Left to her father alone, Charlotte was of the opinion that such objections might soon be over-ruled. Aunt Branwell was the main cause of the trouble. Indeed, what most provoked her niece was the fact "that she reserved the expression of her decided disapproval till all was settled between you and myself . . ."

One must give full marks to Ellen Nussey. One day in

late September she turned up on the Parsonage doorstep with the vehicle that was to take her and Charlotte to Leeds station. There was nothing Aunt Branwell could do about it without being downright ill-mannered. And in that light she would never have allowed herself to appear, certainly not with people of the Nusseys' social standing.

☆   ☆ ☆   ☆

Bridlington (it was called Burlington then) is a picturesque little seaside town, very popular with holiday-makers in the North and the Midlands. It has a fine stretch of sand for the children to play on and the older folk (as one enthusiastically informed me) love nothing better than to see its gabled houses round the quayside and its bow-fronted shops in the narrow High Street " so little changed after all these years . . ."

Historically it counts a great deal in our island story. It was here that Charles Stuart's queen, Henrietta Maria, sought refuge from the ships of the Parliamentary forces and at 5 o'clock one morning was literally bombarded by cannon-shot out of temporary house and home. Off nearby Flamborough Head occurred our one and only engagement with American naval forces in home waters when the notorious Paul Jones made bold to attack a fleet of merchantmen with four comparatively insignificant vessels.

Here too is all that remains of the once famous St. Augustine Priory (in the shape of the original gatehouse and part of the church) which was founded in 1113 and razed to the ground at the Dissolution in 1539. The church is still quite magnificent, more especially since the restoration of its West Front by Sir Gilbert Scott.

In the shade of this church the bodies of some two score sailors lie peacefully at rest between green lawns and over-hanging trees. In the great gale of 1871 a fleet of ships was wrecked on this coast and the local life-boat was smashed to atoms with the loss of most of its own crew. I was told that every year a memorial service is held for them and the present life-boat is paraded ceremoniously through the town.

Charlotte, of course, would have missed all this though she was no doubt well aware of all that had happened here previously. What most involved her, emotionally, was her first sight of the sea. Ellen said later that she had been "quite over-powered" and could not speak of it "till she had shed some tears . . ."

The two girls spent their first fortnight some two miles inland at a farmhouse owned by a family named Hudson in the small hamlet of Easton. Charlotte never forgot these kind people and was continually enquiring about them. I too made it my business to seek out the low whitewashed house with its roof of red tiles, its mantled ivy and rambling wild roses. Alas, I found it had been pulled down as recently as 1961.

☆   ☆ ☆   ☆

Charlotte returned to Haworth at the latter end of October having spent the last week of her holiday with Ellen in lodgings down on the quayside at Bridlington. Like Papa and Aunt Branwell, the Hudsons were not altogether in favour of the two girls wandering round town on their own but they yielded much more gracefully to letting them have their way. What that particular way was is something we can only wonder about.

Back at Haworth there had been much change. Tabitha Aykroyd, the old servant, had been forced through her lameness (occasioned by that fall on the ice) to retire temporarily to a small house in the village which she had bought out of her savings . . . Apart from "a little girl to run errands" (wrote Charlotte to Ellen in December 1839) she and Emily had to do most of the housework on their own. "I manage the ironing, and keep the rooms clean"; (she says) "Emily does the baking, and attends to the cooking." She confesses also to the fact that she "excited aunt's wrath very much by burning the clothes, the first time I attempted to iron; but I do better now."

It is interesting to reflect that the "little girl" engaged to "run errands" was Martha Brown, the sexton's daughter, who was to remain in Mr Bronte's service till his death in 1861 and later accompanied the Rev. Arthur Bell Nicholls (Charlotte's husband) when he returned to his native Ireland.

The greatest change in the Bronte household, however, was the introduction in August 1839 of William Weightman as curate and invaluable assistant to Mr Bronte in the administration of the parish church of St. Michael and All Angels.

He was 25 years old at the time and had just taken his M.A. degree at Durham. "A handsome − clean − prepossessing − good-humoured young man" was how Charlotte described him. He was more. He was a tonic to the Bronte household and indeed to the whole neighbourhood. Everybody liked Willie Weightman − and that included both Mr Bronte and Aunt Branwell.

There was only one flaw in his character, at least so far as Charlotte was concerned. He liked everybody in his turn and most of all any presentable member of the fair sex. If there was ever a more incorrigible flirt there was certainly never one more blissfully ignorant of the fact or more pains-takingly honourable in his intentions.

Charlotte seems to have feared more for her friends on that score than for herself. She continually twitted both Ellen Nussey and Martha Taylor whenever he appeared to cast a favourable eye in their direction and they were equally of the opinion that she 'fancied' him on her own account. No one gave a thought to poor Anne Bronte whom we now have every reason to believe was secretly pining away for him. She had perforce to sublimate her feelings for Willie Weightman by portraying him as the young curate, Mr Weston, who loved and was loved by Agnes Grey. So far as Anne was concerned there was to be no such happy ending.

During the whole of 1840 Willie Weightman continued to be Mr Bronte's constant guide and support in the administration of church affairs and to break feminine hearts everywhere in the process. We read how in February he went out of his way to post separate Valentines from Bradford to all the girls at Haworth Parsonage (including Ellen who was staying there at the time). On another occasion he invited them all to attend a lecture he was giving at the Mechanics' Institute in Keighley and walked the four miles home with them well after midnight to receive hot coffee and a remonstrance from Aunt Branwell who does not appear to have been too much perturbed at having to wait up for them.

Poor Willie Weightman — 'Celia Amelia' as Charlotte loved to call him . . . In a little over two years time he was to die of cholera with a scarcity of young friends near to mourn him. They, in the meantime, were all going their separate ways again and each with the object of earning a living: Branwell, in January 1840 and Charlotte and Anne in March 1841.

☆   ☆ ☆   ☆

Chapter 24

INTERLUDE – BROUGHTON-IN-FURNESS –
SOWERBY BRIDGE – LUDDENDEN FOOT
(January 1840 - April 1842)

AFTER HIS FAILURE to achieve even a modicum of success as a portrait painter in Bradford, Mr Bronte's son and heir returned to the business of writing, with as little to show for it. Indeed, it transpired that none of Branwell's quite voluminous literary work (in the shape of poems and stories) was ever to prove commercially viable. It is interesting only in relation to the more lasting fame his sisters finally achieved and by comparison with the even duller poems his father at least managed to have marketed in volume form.

His undoubted brilliance (and especially when under the influence of drink) was of too evanescent a character to guarantee him any kind of settled livelihood. Nevertheless it was incumbent on him to earn his living somehow. Mr Bronte's resources were not sufficient to keep him in that state of idleness which he had all too often grown accustomed to.

Shamed, perhaps, by his sisters' efforts to fend for themselves (however unsuccessfully) he at last determined to follow their example and, if possible, make a better job of it. At the end of December 1839 he obtained for himself the position of tutor to the family of a Mr Postlethwaite (a country gentleman, fox-hunter, and Justice of the Peace) residing at Broughton House, Broughton-in-Furness, some 10 miles N.W. of Ulverston and, appropriately enough, not far distant from the shores of Lake Windermere (made famous by Wordsworth, Coleridge and De Quincey).

It is interesting to reflect that on the way there from Haworth he must of necessity have passed the site of the old school at Cowan Bridge which had occasioned his family so many bitter memories. One cannot help wondering what his own thoughts must have been at this sudden confrontation and whether or not they put any check on whatever enthusiasm he had whipped up for the adventure on which he was bound.

Certainly it turned out to be a much better proposition than had been offered Charlotte, Emily, and Anne in similar circumstances. The trouble was, being Branwell, he was not able to do justice to it. The rot had already set in before he even arrived at his destination. Having perforce to stay overnight at Kendal he imbibed, not wisely, but only too well and (as he confided in a letter to his old Haworth crony, John Brown, the sexton) "found myself in bed next morning, with a bottle of porter, a glass, and a corkscrew beside me . . ."

His duties at Broughton House were anything but arduous and his employer would appear to have allowed him plenty of free time, too much in fact. Mr Postlethwaite's two sons (John, aged 12 and William, a little over 10) he describes as "fine, spirited lads" and Mrs Postlethwaite seems to have come up to his expectations as being an "amiable wife . . ." He quite obviously got on well with them and met up with none of the problems his sisters had to contend with.

In another letter to his friend, the sexton, he depicts just how admirable his situation was. "I am fixed" (he says) "in a little retired town by the sea-shore, among wild woody hills that rise round me − huge, rocky, and capped with clouds. My employer is a retired country magistrate, a large land-owner, of a right hearty and generous disposition . . . My landlord is a respectable surgeon, and six days out of seven as drunk as a lord . . . I ride to the banker's at Ulverston with Mr Postlethwaite, and sit drinking tea and talking slander with old ladies. As to the young ones! I have one sitting by me just now − fair-faced, blue-eyed, dark-haired, sweet eighteen −she little thinks the devil is so near her!"

This is Branwell 'playing to the gallery' with a vengeance. One cannot possibly imagine him ever being in the position to take advantage of such a situation. But from time immemorial young men have bragged in that way to their friends. If they did not one might well suppose them to be up to all sorts of unmentionable mischief.

Mr Postlethwaite's tutor, unfortunately, was not able to put his imagination to better use. He took more and more time off from his official duties, even going as far afield as Ambleside (in May 1840) on a visit to Hartley Coleridge (eldest son of the famous author of 'The Ancient Mariner') who seems to have been not a little impressed with a translation of the Odes of Horace which Branwell had been engaged on for some time. Mr Postlethwaite, however, was very far from being impressed with his employee's extra-mural activities and in particular with his increasing tendency for taking unauthorised leave of absence. So far as he was concerned that trip to Ambleside was the last straw. He let it be known, in no uncertain terms, that Branwell's services were no longer required.

In June 1840 Mr Bronte's prodigal son returned home once again with as little to show for having left it as on the previous occasion of his London visit. Aunt Branwell's forbearance, in particular, must have been stretched almost to breaking point. Charlotte, Emily, and Anne . . . all seemed to be incapable of sticking to anything for long. But that her 'favourite nephew' should have proved equally as inconsistent . . . It was too much to put up with, more especially by one who conceived 'doing one's duty' as possibly the most important of all Christian virtues.

☆   ☆ ☆   ☆

And now follows perhaps the most surprising of all Branwell's efforts to come to grips with the workaday world he more usually chose to shun away from. On September 29, 1840 Charlotte wrote to her friend Ellen Nussey announcing the fact that "A distant relative of mine, one Patrick Branwell, has set off to seek his fortune in the wild, wandering, adventurous, romantic, knight-errant-like capacity of clerk on the Leeds and Manchester Railroad . . ."

If there appears to be a touch of sarcasm here (even a

hint of snobbishness) it was probably not meant. Charlotte may have meant all she said but what she said could not possibly have conveyed half what she must have thought. It was her way to romanticise any given situation and she was obviously doing her best with this one.

Branwell, in fact, had somehow managed to secure for himself the post of Assistant Clerk in Charge at Sowerby Bridge Station, near Halifax (on a new stretch of line between Hebden Bridge and Leeds) at a salary of £75 a year.

With all due respects to railway clerks, past and present, this would seem to be the last job on earth for a young man of Branwell's pretentions and inclinations. It must be taken into consideration, however, that railways were then a comparatively new and booming industry. Large fortunes were being made and lost by fast operators and shareholders and the Bronte family themselves had speculated a little of their sparse capital on the opening up of new lines of communication which they fondly hoped might lead to the proverbial crock of gold at the end of the rainbow or at least some daylight at the end of a long tunnel. In this respect they may well have regarded Branwell's comparatively mean occupation as a 'knight-errant-like' one. There was no telling at what station in life it might end.

Sowerby Bridge Station was certainly no Waterloo. It was only opened at the beginning of October 1840 and then mainly for the passage of goods traffic to and from the neighbouring mills. The 'office' Branwell occupied with his account books and time tables was no more than a wooden and corrugated-iron shack. It still forms part of the present-day goods yard or at least it did, last time I was there.

As 'Assistant Clerk in Charge' Branwell appears to have had plenty of time to ruminate over his future prospects there being no more than half-a-dozen or so trains passing through every day. As a consequence, most of his ruminating was done in the local pubs (of which there were plenty) and the only up-hill work he encountered was the constant and possibly unsteady climb up Sowerby Street which was not unlike the cobbled approach to the

Parsonage at Haworth. He was also lucky enough to be not far from Halifax and the many friends he had made there, including Leyland, the sculptor. It was handy for spending the occasional convivial evening.

Nevertheless, his time was obviously not completely wasted for on April 1st 1841 (only six months after taking up his first appointment) his employers saw fit to promote him to the position of Clerk in Charge at Luddenden Foot, the next station up the line, at an increased salary of £130. A most propitious step forward, on the face of it, though as things turned out they might have been better advised to leave him where he was.

☆   ☆ ☆   ☆

Luddenden Foot is linked by a tunnel with Sowerby Bridge but Branwell can hardly be said to have come out into the clear at the other end. In fact things ended for him in a bigger muddle than ever before.

No doubt his increased responsibility (as station-master, with one porter to assist him) proved more than he was able to manage. Traffic was heavier, for one thing, and the necessary accounting system much more involved. As a consequence, and being the man he was, Branwell found more and more occasion to neglect his duties. He was also in the position of being able to delegate most of them to someone else.

Luddenden Foot too was not unlike his native Haworth, its main street straggling up to a small square and church with its chief inn, the Lord Nelson, occupying much the same position as the Black Bull at home. Needless to say he spent much time there and availed himself of the opportunity it presented of borrowing books from its remarkable and justly famous circulating library. There too he met, and no doubt often caroused with, Francis Henry Grundy (an engineer on the same line) who was later to record his reminiscencies of Branwell in a book called "Pictures of the Past" which he published in 1879. "Poor, brilliant, gay, moody, moping, wildly excitable, miserable Bronte!" was how he graphically described him.

Meanwhile, back at the station, Branwell's assistant was busy cooking the books (or so we are to assume). When (at the end of 1841) the annual accounts were audited there was found to be a discrepancy of £11-1-7d. It was also found that Branwell had whiled away a fair proportion of the firm's time by executing little sketches and scribbling poems in the margins of the ledgers so produced.

So far as concerned the Manchester & Leeds Railway it was no saving grace that some of these poems had been published in the Halifax Guardian. Branwell had been employed by them in an altogether different capacity and if he could be said to have succeeded in some ways as a poet he had almost certainly failed in discharging his duties as Clerk in Charge at Luddenden Foot.

As a consequence, on March 31st 1842, Branwell was informed that his services in that capacity were no longer required. He was considered lucky to have got off so lightly.

☆   ☆ ☆   ☆

Chapter 25

INTERLUDE – UPPERWOOD HOUSE, RAWDON
(March 1841 - December 1841)

AS IF SHE had not had enough punishment, Charlotte volunteered for more when she engaged herself as governess to Mr and Mrs White at Upperwood House, Rawdon, near Bradford on 2nd March, 1841.

Writing to Ellen Nussey just after her arrival she said, "In taking this place I have made a large sacrifice in the way of salary in the hope of securing comfort . . . My pupils are two in number, a girl of eight and a boy of six."

Her salary, in fact, was a mere £20 a year out of which she had to pay £4 for her washing, but the advantages in the way of 'comfort' were quite considerable and certainly an improvement on what she had experienced with the Sidgwicks at Stonegappe. Mr White was a Bradford merchant who, to some extent, had come up the hard way, and his wife preened herself in the wake of his success. Charlotte described them as a "good sort of people" but (true to form) could not resist adding that her pupils were "wild and unbroken, but apparently well disposed."

If she had to continue earning her living, and there was no doubt about that, she could have done much worse than forego some pecuniary advantage for the privilege of working for the Whites at Upperwood House. Nevertheless, she had "enough to do to keep a good heart in the matter." Mr White, she confessed to liking well enough but she soon found herself in the position of "trying hard to like" Mrs White. She could well believe, she said, that her employer had once been "an exciseman's daughter." When put out of her way she could be "highly offensive". Indeed, on one occasion, she provoked Charlotte to the extent of declaring, "She must not give me any more of the same sort – or I shall ask for my wages and go . . ."

There was one very good reason why she did not do so and was prepared indeed to stay with the Whites until the following Christmas. It was no doubt on that account that she was able to admit later that "during the whole of the last six months they only made too much of me."

Charlotte, in fact, had one particular iron in the fire with which she was prepared to smooth out all the Bronte family's immediate difficulties.

☆   ☆ ☆   ☆

It was fairly obvious by this time that none of the girls could be said to have made a success of anything they had set their hands to and though Branwell appeared to be making the best of a bad job it was certainly not one for which he was suited by nature or temperament. The truth of the matter was that none of them were prepared to accept authority but all had a suppressed desire to wield it. This was particularly the case with Charlotte as being the oldest and perhaps the most conscious of her superiority.

Her idea it was that they should start a school of their own and not be constantly at the beck and call of irascible employers in conducting the proper education of their pupils. During the summer holidays of 1841 the matter was discussed at family level and all seemed to be agreed that it might work. Even Mr Bronte and Aunt Branwell were enthusiastic enough to lend their moral support, as well they might be. The problem of what to do with their unsettled and unsettling family was as much their's as anybody elses.

Of course, to start such a venture, the first requisite was capital and they quite literally had not a bean between them. This was typical of Charlotte's reckoning in such matters; she, like her brother, was inclined to act first on impulse and then to find ways and means of squaring the circle. Luckily (some might say surprisingly) Aunt Branwell declared herself willing to come to their assistance with a loan from the little money she had managed to accumulate during her long spinsterhood. In this respect it must be remembered that she had regularly been receiving an annuity of £50 since the death of her parents and she had necessarily found little use for it in the closed society she had been forced to keep at Haworth.

Another surprising (and propitious) offer came from Miss Wooler, Charlotte's former friend and teacher at Roe Head and Dewsbury Moor. Since moving her school to the latter location things had not prospered at all according to plan. She was prepared to let the girls take over the running of it, she said, if they thought there was a possibility of making it a going concern.

It was a tempting and timely proposition and if the girls had taken it up there and then who knows that it might not have succeeded, if only in a modest way. The idea was even approved by Mrs White, Charlotte's employer and Emily (the last of the family to be enthusiastic about such mundane notions) confided to her 4-yearly diary paper that before the next one fell due she might well conceive them as "merrily seated in our own sitting-room in some pleasant and flourishing seminary, having just gathered in for the midsummer holyday . . ." Only Anne appeared to have any doubts on the matter. "Nothing is settled about it yet," she wrote, "and we do not know if we shall be able to or not. I hope we shall . . ."

Anne was right, as it turned out. The proposed school at Dewsbury Moor did not materialise, but not for any reason that had been envisaged when first they prepared their plans. What changed the whole course of their lives was a letter received by Charlotte from an entirely unexpected quarter of the globe.

☆ ☆ ☆ ☆

Mary Taylor, the more intellectual of Charlotte's two school friends at Roe Head was on holiday in Brussels visiting her sister Martha (the happy-go-lucky one) who was finishing her education at a boarding-school there. The picture she painted of the gay European capital and its surroundings and the advantages to be gained from the training in foreign languages that a seminary of that kind might offer to anyone who proposed opening a school of their own, completely fired Charlotte's imagination. Writing to Ellen Nussey in August (whilst still working for Mrs White at Rawdon) she had to confess — "I hardly know what swelled to my throat as I read her (Mary's) letter — such a vehement impatience of restraint and steady work. Such a strong wish for wings . . ."

The upshot was that Charlotte wrote a long letter to Aunt Branwell pointing out (very tactfully and very skilfully) all the wonderful prospects for the future that might be opened to them were her money to be invested in furthering such a scheme. Emily, she suggested, might accompany her if "only for a single half year". Anne (of course) "might take her turn at some future period . . ." The expenditure of £50 or £100 might well be considered as a sprat to catch a mackerel. Then, rather craftily, one must admit, she drew her aunt's attention to the fact that when Papa "left Ireland to go to Cambridge University, he was as ambitious as I am now . . ."

The latter shaft certainly struck home in one direction and who else but Mr Bronte could have been more pricked to the heart by it? The fact remains that Charlotte's plea succeeded. All that remained now was to make the necessary arrangements.

Only Anne was to be cheated out of a share in this new venture. After the Christmas holidays, when plans for their journey were still being eagerly discussed by her two sisters, she returned to the dreary business of being a governess with the Robinson family at Thorp Green, an occupation she had first taken up in the previous March. Later she was to be joined there by Branwell but at the moment no one seems to have been particularly concerned about his prospects. He had not yet 'gone off the track' (so to speak) in his "knight-errant-like capacity of clerk on the Leeds and Manchester Railroad . . ."

☆　　　☆ ☆　　　☆

Chapter 26

INTERLUDE – BRUSSELS
(February 1842 - January 1844)

CHARLOTTE RESIGNED her appointment with the White family at Upperwood House at the end of the year 1841 but it was not until the following February that arrangements were completed for the reception of her and her sister Emily at the Pensionnat of Madame Heger in the Rue d'Isabelle, Brussels.

This excellent establishment had been recommended to Mr Bronte by a mutual friend and fellow-clergyman living not far from Haworth whose brother happened to be the representative British Chaplain in the Belgium capital. The wife of this chaplain, Mrs Jenkins, instituted enquiries about this particular school and put Charlotte in touch with the Heger family. Reasonable terms having been agreed to the girls set out for Brussels on Tuesday, 8th February, accompanied by their father and Mary Taylor and her brother Joe (both of whom had made the journey on previous occasions).

It took them the better part of that day travelling between Leeds and London by rail, a fact which does much to vindicate modern inter-city transport. They then found they were not able to catch a boat (from London Bridge to Ostend) until the following Saturday and had perforce to put up at the (inevitable) Chapter Coffee House in Paternoster Row where, in turn, both Mr Bronte and Branwell had stayed before them. The intervening time was spent in seeing the sights of London, in particular its art galleries and museums. Poor Branwell had followed much the same route but in far less hopeful circumstances.

The combined river and sea journey to Ostend took them another two days and they were then faced with a further full day's travel by stage-coach to Brussels and an overnight stay in a hotel before presenting themselves at the Pensionnat Heger on the following morning. In all the journey had taken them at least a week . . .

Today you can make a (non-passport) return trip across the Channel by hovercraft in the form of a day excursion, the difference being that it will cost you twice as much as it cost the Brontes. Indeed, according to Winifred Gerin (in her biography of Charlotte) the complete journey from London to Brussels in 1842 involved an expenditure of "between £5 and £6, according to the class travelled." However, taking into account the girls' comparatively limited resources, this would have meant a great deal more in terms of our modern (over-inflated) currency. One should remember also that it cost 1/6d to despatch a letter from Haworth to the Belgium capital, near enough the equivalent of today's 8½p post.

☆   ☆ ☆   ☆

Much that happened to Charlotte during her journey to and residence in the Pensionnat Heger is chronicled in her novels 'The Professor' and 'Villette'. They are both, to some extent, as truly autobiographical as what she recorded of her brief stay at Cowan Bridge (the 'Lowood School' of the opening chapters of 'Jane Eyre').

Altogether different, however, was the 'finishing' school for girls run by Mme Héger in the Rue d'Isabelle. Even Charlotte had to admit to the excellence of its curriculum, its almost benign supervision, and its first-class table d'hote. In many respects it was not unlike a comfortable boarding-house or a family-run hotel. Then, of course, there was the added attraction of M. Constantin Heger, Charlotte's French master, who was also one of the professors employed at the adjacent boys' school, the Athenee Royal. That she fell in love with him eventually (if not from the start) we have no reason to doubt. Compare Lucy Snowe's ill-concealed admiration for Paul Emanuel, his counterpart in 'Villette. It is no less certain that his conduct towards her was at all times strictly honourable and correct − much to her long-lasting regret.

Emily made no such record of her stay in Brussels. Indeed, she rarely commented on anything that occurred to her outside the confines of her parsonage home (to which she was always only too anxious to return). All we know of her whilst quartered in the Rue d'Isabelle is that she appears to have been considerably less popular than her sister Charlotte though far and away the more promising pupil. M. Heger, in particular, was much struck by her capabilities, especially in the matter of French translation and composition. One cannot help thinking that if she had really put herself out to please him she might have fared a lot better than Charlotte in his estimation. Emily, however, never put herself out in that way. M. Heger may well have had some of the attributes of Paul Emanuel and a little of Mr Rochester in his composition. So far as Emily was concerned he was certainly no Heathcliffe.

☆   ☆ ☆   ☆

I cannot believe that Madame Heger herself in any way qualified for the caricature Charlotte drew of her in the person of Madame Beck. That she had some inkling of Charlotte's feelings towards her husband I do not doubt but I don't think it was in her nature to betray her suspicions quite so obviously as she is made to do in 'Villette'. I think she would have much preferred to let things ride and for events to take their natural course.

Both the Hégers were for long years highly respected in the community and Madame Héger, in particular, had enough to do in efficiently running her respectable establishment and bringing up her own family of three very young girls (later added to by 2 sons and another daughter) without worrying unduly about the influence on her husband of so patently plain and unattractive a pupil. If he was to be tempted at all from the path of virtue he must have felt she had least to fear in the person of Charlotte.

Indeed, she went out of her way to be accommodating towards her, even to the extent of inviting her to share the family sitting-room during after-duty hours on account of

Charlotte's obvious loneliness (an invitation which, needless to say, was rebuffed). It was Madame Héger, too, who patiently pieced together the torn-up correspondence which Charlotte later persistently and unavailingly addressed to her husband, thus unwittingly bequeathing details of the so-called 'affair' for Posterity to gape at.

That Charlotte disliked her is certain, but equally she had little affection for any of her fellow-pupils or teachers. In a letter to Ellen Nussey (written only shortly after she arrived at the Pensionnat) she remarked of the Belgians that if their national character was to be "measured by the character of most of the girls in this school, it is a character singularly cold, selfish, animal, and inferior. They are very mutinous and difficult for the teachers to manage; and their principles are rotten to the core . . ." She was also of the opinion that, in general, the Belgians hated the English.

It was an attitude to be expected of one who had been brought up to respect strictly Protestant traditions and found herself one of a small minority among a host of Roman Catholics. The same bias appears in most of her writing. Also the insularity of her situation in Haworth whose inhabitants considered as 'foreigners' all who lived beyond their boundaries inclined to force her mind into a narrow groove in that respect. In 'Villette' (for instance) when reflecting on her stay at the Chapter Coffee House she describes the Cockney dialect as "odd as a foreign tongue." "I had never before heard the English language chopped up in that way," she says. I have heard much the same sentiments expressed by Southerners about anyone living north of Oxford and the reverse is undoubtedly just as true.

Charlotte, at least, had the grace to acknowledge that Brussels was a "beautiful" city but she had in mind mainly the nobility of its architecture in the shape of its 15th century Hotel de Ville, the church of Ste. Gudule (where she once actually made 'confession' to a Roman Catholic priest), and the Maison du Roi in the Grande Place (then, as now, one of the most attractive public squares in Europe). Though the school in the Rue d'Isabelle has long been swept away by the tide of modern development she would have little difficulty in recognising all these landmarks including the central park where she described herself as wandering lonely among the gaily-dressed crowds, listening to music, and admiring the frequent firework displays. What she would make of modern Brussels is another matter. With its fashionable shops, its smart (and expensive) restaurants and its 'trendy' night-spots it is indeed a "boom town" and comparable in every way with Paris and Berlin. For this one can either praise or blame the Common Market (according to one's opinion about that modern innovation). It continues to remain the headquarters of the European Economic Community — and there I doubt if Charlotte would have felt very much at home. She would no doubt have seen this conglomeration of individual states as the final triumph of the Napoleonic ideal over her childhood hero, Wellington.

In any case she had very little time for either trade or tradesmen.

☆   ☆ ☆   ☆

It was originally planned that Charlotte and Emily should return to Haworth in September 1842 but Madame Heger persuaded them (and the family at home) that they should temporarily become members of the teaching staff whilst continuing their studies free of charge (another instance of her disinterestedness in-so-far as it concerned Charlotte's influence on her husband, or vice-versa).

Death again intervened to upset these arrangements, as so often had been the case in the past. First came the news that poor Willie Weightman had been struck down by cholera with only Branwell to mourn for him (openly) at the funeral. Then, only shortly afterwards, little Martha Taylor (who had been the life of the party at Roe Head) succumbed to the same complaint whilst continuing to attend school out at Koekelburg (a North-Western suburb of Brussels) and was buried in the Protestant Cemetery on the Chaussea de Louvres. Finally (in November) they received the even more startling news that Aunt Branwell had been taken seriously ill and by the next post that she had failed to recover from what appears to have been some intestinal complaint. They rushed back home immediately, but in consequence of taking the wrong route, arrived too late for the funeral. It was the final indignity poor Elizabeth Branwell was called upon to suffer . . .

Though M. Héger strongly recommended to Mr Bronte that both girls should be allowed to return to the Rue d'Isabelle, only Charlotte was prepared to take him up on it. Emily had had more than enough but in this particular instance her sister persisted in being a glutton for punishment. It was sufficient consolation for her increased loneliness and sense of isolation that she was assigned to instructing her idol in the intricacies of the English language. She wanted only that he should penetrate more deeply in to its capacity for expressing the poetry of romance.

She had once described M. Héger to her friend Ellen as "very choleric and irritable in temperament; a little black being, with a face that varies in expressions. Sometimes he borrows the lineaments of an insane tom-cat, sometimes those of a delirious hyena . . ." At the same she almost swooned with delight whenever he showed her the least sign of approbation. That she 'had it bad' (as we say) is obvious.

Without Emily's company (and correcting commonsense) to fall back on she inclined more and more to indulge in this wildly improbable day-dream. At the same time she made every effort to counteract any possible misinterpretation that might be put on it by her friends and acquaintances. In a letter to Ellen (dated 1st April 1843) she strenuously denies any rumour that she may have returned to Brussels with the object of obtaining some mythical husband. That she had turned down a prospective salary of £50 per annum in England for one of only £16 in Belgium had nothing to do with it, she protested. Alas, she protested too much.

The outcome should have been obvious from the start, though in our own time it might well have ended much less satisfactorily for all parties concerned. Madame Héger *did*, eventually, become more than a little suspicious of what was going on. Her first step was to put a stop to her husband's 'English lessons', then (on one pretext or another) to remove him as far as possible from Charlotte's personal sphere of influence. Charlotte reacted by giving in her notice which was the only way she had previously been able to deal with Miss Wooler and Mrs Sidgwick. She could put up with anything but the thought of being unjustly slighted and then woe-betide anyone who roused her temper.

M. Héger would have none of it, at first, but only because he valued Charlotte's services as a teacher. Had there been any other reason he would not have submitted so tamely eventually to the fact that she might after all be spared. Charlotte packed her bags and left Brussels for good on the 1st January 1844. All she obtained by way of satisfaction from the master she idolised was a few books he had given her as gifts and a diploma recording the excellence of her qualifications . . .

☆   ☆ ☆   ☆

Chapter 27

INTERLUDE – THORP GREEN HALL,
LITTLE OUSEBURN, Nr YORK
(March 1841 - July 1845)

IT WOULD SEEM to have been poor Anne Bronte's misfortune that whilst her sisters Charlotte and Emily were (in general) given the opportunity of doing what they wanted to do (whether or not they made the most of it) she was the one committed to the almost continual drudgery of uncongenial employment. To her was consigned the main share of the proverbial donkey-work.

And like her heroine, Agnes Grey, she set out on each new venture with renewed optimism and was the last to complain when disillusionment forced her to retire. When, at the latter end of March 1841, she accepted the post of governess with the Robinson family at Thorp Green, some 12 miles from the cathedral city of York, she had no idea how disastrously her long period of employment there (i.e., until the summer of 1845) was to be concluded. She had her brother to thank for that, who (least of all the family) was prepared to keep his nose to the grindstone with any prospect of success.

Mr Robinson was what is known as a "hunting" parson (a common enough phenomenon in those days). His wife (later immortalised as 'Mrs Murray' in 'Agnes Grey) was by all accounts an extremely attractive woman and in consequence, socially conscious of the fact and given to entertaining in the accepted fashionable style. They had three daughters, Lydia, Elizabeth and Mary (later portrayed as constitutionally lazy and thoughtless rather than downright objectionable). Edmund (their only son) was undoubtedly a 'bit of a handful' which is probably why Branwell eventually arrived on the scene to give him the benefit of his own experience in that respect.

Thorp Green Hall (the family mansion) was a "large
house with long windows descending to the ground" and
situated among rolling acres of cultivated land. Nothing
remains of it today but the stables and part of the domestic premises, the mansion (as such) having been destroyed
by fire at the beginning of this century. Mrs Gaskell would
no doubt have applauded the fact as the work of Divine
Justice. She never had a good word for its having been
built in the first place and was even more scathing about
its inhabitants, in particular Mrs Robinson with whom she
almost became involved in a law-suit. "A depraved
woman," she called her, and again — "her taste must have
been as depraved as her principles."

But of that, and the occasion that appeared to warrant
it, I will have more to say later.

☆   ☆ ☆   ☆

In spite of the fact that Anne (in common with her
sisters) had some difficulty in instructing her pupils in the
so-called fine arts (their mother being mainly concerned
with their being trained to take up some future position in
'high society' via the social graces of singing, dancing and
riding to hounds) she appears to have been comparatively
happy during her first period of service with the
Robinsons. There were compensations in the occasional
trips to York and accompanying the family on their annual
visit to Scarborough, a place she came to love almost more
than any other, mainly on account of the sea. It was in
that setting that she arranged for her heroine, Agnes Grey,
to be proposed to by her hero, Mr Weston.

On Sundays (whilst at Thorp Green) she regularly
worshipped at the nearby church of the Holy Trinity at
Little Ouseburn, trailing always at some distance behind
her master and mistress and occasionally being graciously
permitted to occupy the same carriage with them,
although, in truth, they were all bound for the same final
destination where no account is presumably taken of
wealth or rank. That no one deigned to acknowledge her

presence on these expeditions is proof enough that although 'with them' she was most certainly not 'of them.'

If anything comforted her at all during this period it was that Charlotte's intention of running their own school might not turn out after all to be an impossible dream. There was even a possibility that things might come right between her and her favourite among Mr Bronte's curates in the way of all that was best in romantic fiction of the time. She was to be disappointed in both cases, or might it not be truer to say that life dealt with her as, secretly, she reasoned it would?

Apart from Branwell, she was the most hard done by of all the Bronte family. Unlike her brother, however, she accepted it with that patient resignation which was so much a part of her nature.

☆   ☆ ☆   ☆

Branwell, of course, merely blundered on from one crisis to another and railed the more bitterly not so much against fate as against his own inability to stand up to and overcome it. Charlotte fought back; Emily was completely indifferent; Anne endured. Branwell, possessing none of these qualities, simply succumbed.

Having been sacked from his position at Luddendon Foot he made a few half-hearted attempts to obtain a situation more suited to the talents he supposed himself to possess. It was on Anne's suggestion (and obviously agreed to by the Robinsons) that after the Christmas holidays of 1842 he accompanied her back to Thorp Green as prospective tutor to Mr Robinson's only son, Edmund. It was quite outside Anne's province to deal with the lad and it was reasonable to suppose that having had some experience of that kind in the household of Mr Postlethwaite at Broughton-in-Furness Branwell might well be able to adapt himself to a similar situation.

References were obviously not called for. Otherwise he would most certainly not have been engaged and everybody would have been the happier for it.

That he must have given some satisfaction is proved by

the fact that he managed to remain at Thorp Green for some two and a half years (i.e., from January 1843 to July 1845). It is said that from the start he was fascinated by his employer's wife as being the only "real lady" he had ever been called upon to have dealings with. What she felt about him is still doubtful but that in some way or other he impressed her with his fatal "Irish charm" may be deduced from the fact that she continued to tolerate him for so long. Mr Robinson is reported as having openly sneered at his artistic pretentions, having little inclination himself for pursuits of that kind. When not confined to his bed (which on account of poor health was frequently the case) he much preferred to be at full gallop with a pack of hounds after the elusive fox.

In consequence Mrs Robinson and Branwell had too often to rely on each other's company and with her more cultural inclinations it was not to be wondered at that she was fascinated, if not enamoured, by the obviously clever and poetical young tutor, some 17 years her junior. Nor was the fact overlooked by her children, in particular her three daughters (all of whom at that time were well into their teens and not entirely unacquainted with the facts of life). Even Edmund (the youngest member of the family) though only 11 years old was not unaware of what was going on. Anne (in the guise of "Master Charles" in Agnes Grey) described him as not being able to "read correctly the easiest line in the simplest book" and as "only active in doing mischief, and only clever in inventing falsehoods." Such a child could, and must, have proved a menace to whatever Branwell Bronte and Lydia Robinson had in mind for each other's consolation.

When Anne and her brother came home for their summer holidays in June 1845 Charlotte (who had returned from Brussels some 18 months previously) noted, with some relief, that her sister had no intention of returning to her employment at Thorp Green. She noted also that her brother was moody, irritable, and ill at ease and that he could not get back fast enough to rejoin the Robinsons (at that time on holiday in Scarborough).

Anne said nothing at that juncture though it was pretty

plain later that she knew just how affairs were progressing with the Robinson family and had no wish to take any further part in them. That the children were by this time busy blackmailing both her and their mother into getting their own way in everything under threat of exposing everything to Papa is now quite certain. Whether they did so or Mrs Robinson herself (and as a safeguard for her future prospects) confessed the whole matter to her husband, laying emphasis on the fact that Branwell was chiefly to blame in the affair, we shall never know. The fact remains that Branwell, before ever reaching Scarborough via Thorp Green, got a letter of dismissal from his employer. A rider was added to the effect that should he ever dare to show his face in the vicinity again he would be shot on sight.

Charlotte, returning to Haworth from a brief holiday in Derbyshire with Ellen Nussey, found her brother unexpectedly at home and looking "very sick." In all probability, by that, she meant that he was either dead drunk or under the influence of drugs — or both. It was a tendency towards which he was ever afterwards to be drawn.

Anne told all, of course. There was no reason now why she should not. One can only reflect that the most shaken was probably the old man (in the unavoidable absence of his once favourite aunt). Charlotte's only comment (in a letter to Ellen) was that they had had "sad work with Branwell. He thought of nothing but stunning or drowning his agony of mind. No one in this house could have rest . . ."

Emily kept her own counsel, as usual. We will never know what she felt about the matter. I am of the opinion that she was the only one in the whole sorry affair who had any real sympathy or understanding of what it means to be the 'odd man out' in a smug and hypocritical world. She was the nearest to him in that respect.

☆ ☆ ☆ ☆

Chapter 28

HAWORTH (July 1845 - July 1848)

AT THE TOP of Main Street, Haworth, there are three poignant reminders of the Brontes' residence there. They are the Black Bull Hotel (which, after his dismissal by Mr Robinson, Branwell took to frequenting more often than ever before); the Druggist's shop, where he obtained (quite easily) ever increasing doses of laudanum; and (on the opposite side of the road) the post office and stationers where the three sisters purchased their writing paper and from which they despatched the manuscripts of their poems and novels to their London publishers.

I recall, whilst staying in the neighbourhood recently, being approached by an earnest-looking young man with a strong Mid-west accent. It was just after ten on a Saturday morning and the crowd outside the Black Bull, waiting for the bars to open, was quite remarkable. They were not necessarily there for the beer.

"Excuse me," he said, "but this *is* the pub where Branwell used to get drunk and take opium, isn't it?" I said he certainly imbibed more than was good for him there, on occasion, but so far as I knew he was not in the habit of indulging both vices at the same time and under the same roof. His face literally took fire with enthusiasm, though I can't say I altogether approved of his particular line of enquiry.

The three girls, indeed, had a pretty bad time with their brother; the more so when he finally realised that Lydia Robinson (his erstwhile lady-love) had no intention of continuing their illicit relationship, even after her husband's death. Writing to Ellen Nussey, on August 18th 1845, Charlotte remarks (somewhat caustically) "My hopes ebb low indeed about Branwell. I sometimes fear he will never be fit for much. The late blow to his prospects

and feelings has quite made him reckless. It is only abso-
lute want of means that acts as any check to him."

Want of means certainly did not deter him from wheedl-
ing every penny he could out of both his father and Mrs
Robinson, by what can only be described as a form of
moral blackmail. Mrs Gaskell says "For some time before
his death he had attacks of delirium tremens of the most
frightful character; he slept in his father's room, and he
would sometimes declare that either he or his father
should be dead before morning . . . In the mornings young
Bronte would saunter out, saying, with a drunkard's incon-
tinence of speech, 'The poor old man and I have had a
terrible night of it; he does his best − the poor old man!
but it's all over with me;' (whimpering) 'it's *her* fault, her
fault.' " A frightful state of affairs, indeed, though only
Charlotte would appear to have completely damned him
for it. Anne (in one of her diary papers, dated 30th July
1845) simply refers to his having had "much tribulation
and ill-health." Emily (in her corresponding diary paper)
hopes that he "will be better and do better hereafter . . ."

☆   ☆ ☆   ☆

Charlotte, of course, was still smarting from the
supposed indifference of her former French master,
Constantin Heger, to her own feelings. In the circumstances one might have expected her to show a little more
forbearance in the somewhat similar case of her brother
and Lydia Robinson. Maybe it was because *she* had not
yielded to temptation and Branwell had. There is no prude
quite like one who has been thwarted by lack of opportunity.

Nevertheless, long after Branwell had resigned himself to
his hopeless situation, she persisted in badgering M. Heger
with self-pitying letters to which there could be no satis-
factory answer. He replied more and more brusquely as
time went on and finally dried up altogether. What
possible consolation could be offered to one who admitted
to finding neither rest nor peace, day or night, on account
of not having heard from him? "Monsieur," (she wrote)

"the poor have not need of much to sustain them — they ask only for the crumbs that fall from the rich man's table. But if they are refused the crumbs they die of hunger . . ." At their best such communications were merely pathetic; at their worst, downright embarrassing.

We have no reason to regard M. Heger as anything but a loving husband and affectionate father. As for his wife, Zoe, (unjustly libelled as 'Madame Beck' in Charlotte's novel, 'Villette) she was so far convinced of her husband's innocence in the so-called "affaire" that she pains-takingly pieced together Charlotte's letters which he had casually (if not crossly) ripped apart and later bequeathed them to her son for disposal as he thought fit. He in turn bequeathed them to the British Museum in 1913.

M. Heger's letters to Charlotte would appear to have been destroyed completely, whether by their recipient or someone else (having no wish the correspondence should come to light) we shall never know. Certainly, Mrs Gaskell soft-pedalled on the whole business. For one thing, she didn't want another law-suit on her hands. For another, it was anything but politic to give offence to Charlotte's husband, the Rev. Arthur Bell Nicholls. He had only grudgingly given his consent to her writing his wife's biography, anyway.

The subject is still matter for endless debate. It is no more likely to be settled than anything concerning the personal relationships of two people long since unable to speak for themselves.

☆ ☆ ☆ ☆

Charlotte had known many black periods in her life and the period immediately following her return from Brussels was one of the blackest. Quite apart from the trouble Branwell was causing the whole family, the school project the girls had so set their hearts on proved, in the words of Emily, to be "no go." The sisters had gone to the trouble and expense of printing and circulating a prospectus for "The Misses Bronte's Establishment for The Board and Education of a limited number of Young Ladies at The

Parsonage, Haworth, Near Bradford." Not a single person presented herself for such instruction. No one, it seemed, was the least interested.

Well, you know what they say? It's an ill wind, etc., etc. . . . Had the Parsonage School House become a flourishing concern we should obviously never have read the biographical notice of her sisters which Charlotte was later to write for the edition of "Wuthering Heights and Agnes Grey" published in 1850.

"One day in the autumn of 1845" (she said) "I accidentlly lighted on a MS volume of verse, in my sister Emily's hand-writing . . . I looked it over and something more than surprise seized me — a deep conviction that these were not common effusions, nor at all like the poetry women generally write. I thought them condensed and terse, vigorous and genuine. To my ear they had also a peculiar music, wild, melancholy, and elevating . . ."

Charlotte thought them worthy of publication but she had a job both in convincing and reconciling Emily to the fact. No doubt Emily was fully aware of their intrinsic merit, but writing was a purely personal matter with her. She deeply resented her privacy being so rudely disturbed.

That she agreed eventually was no doubt only because Charlotte and Anne wished to be involved in the venture. She may also have been stung into retaliation by her elder sister's somewhat condescending attitude to her younger sister's poems. "I could not but be a partial judge," Charlotte wrote later, "yet I thought that these verses too had a sweet sincere pathos of their own." The operative word here is "sweet". Emily would have inclined to be most bitter about that. She loved Anne more than anyone else in the world and mainly on account of their long and close association with the Gondal chronicles.

It was finally agreed that a small selection of the sister's poems should be submitted for publication under the pseudonyms 'Currer, Ellis, and Acton Bell.' "The ambiguous choice", said Charlotte, was "dictated by a sort of conscientious scruple of assuming Christian names, positively masculine, while we did not like to declare ourselves women, because — without at the time suspecting that our mode of writing and thinking was not what is called "feminine", — we had a vague impression that authoresses are liable to be looked on with prejudice."

It mattered little in the long run under what names they chose to present their poetry to an unappreciative public. "The bringing out of our little book was hard work," Charlotte confessed. "As was to be expected" (and note that phrase in particular as saying so much about Charlotte's character), "neither we nor our poems were at all wanted ... The great puzzle lay in the difficulty of getting answers of any kind from the publishers to whom we applied ..."

Eventually it was suggested (by Messrs Chambers of Edinburgh) that the firm of Aylott & Jones (of Paternoster Row) might be inclined to undertake production of the work, specialising as they did in poetry of a 'religious' nature. They *were* indeed, but not at their own risk. The slim volume, ("a thinner volume than I had anticipated", said Charlotte), containing 21 poems each by Emily and Anne and 19 by Charlotte, "stole into life" (according to Mrs Gaskell) "about the end of May, 1846 ... without the mighty murmuring public discovering that three more voices were uttering their speech ..." It sold at 4/- (20p) a copy and the Bronte sisters contributed some £40 towards the cost of its production. *Two copies only were sold.*

Few periodicals of the time bothered to review it. Only the Athenæum would appear to have been at all far-sighted as to its merit. They assigned to 'Ellis' (i.e., Emily) "the highest rank of the three 'brothers' " and referred to her as possessing "an evident power of wing that may reach heights not here attempted." In this not too ungracious manner they dismissed one of the finest women poets of all time.

I can't help thinking that had the sisters dared to issue the work under their own names they might well have sold a not unreasonable number of copies, if only to friends and acquaintances. Outside the family circle, however, no one was aware they had printed a single line; not even Ellen Nussey, who might be said to have been the most closely concerned with their welfare.

Undaunted by their lack of success (as all true writers must be) the three sisters were already "preparing for the press a work of fiction, consisting of three distinct and unconnected tales which may be published either together, as a work of three volumes, of the ordinary novel size, or separately, as single volumes, as may be deemed most advisable." The three works were "Wuthering Heights," "Agnes Grey," and "The Professor."

Aylott & Jones were prepared to publish nothing of that kind but they were not averse to recommending likely competitors for the privilege. For well over a year the three novels were alternately submitted and rejected. Some of our own 'best-selling' authors have had much the same experience.

As if Charlotte had not worries enough she had now to concern herself with her father's health. His eyesight was threatened by the formation of a cataract. If action was not taken soon he was likely to end up completely blind.

At the end of July 1846 (just after the publication of the poems) Charlotte and Emily (as related by Mrs Gaskell) "made a jorney to Manchester for the purpose of searching out an operator; and there they heard of the fame of the late Mr Wilson as an oculist." On seeking him out, however, he was unable to advise them without first seeing the prospective patient. Accordingly, about a month later, Charlotte brought her father to Manchester where they took temporary lodgings at No. 83 Mount Pleasant (off the Oxford Road), described by Mrs Gaskell as being "in one of numerous similar streets of small monotonous-looking houses, in a suburb of the town."

Mrs Gaskell might well have been acquainted with it. She herself was living in Manchester at the time, though in a much more select area. She knew nothing of the Brontes, however, and in consequence had even less concern for them. Neither had the Nazis, presumably. The whole area was destroyed during the Blitz.

The operation was successfully carried out on 26th August and on that same day Charlotte's novel, "The Professor", landed with a sickening thud on the doormat of their back-street lodgings, rejected for the umpteenth time. Almost without turning a hair Charlotte resolutely sat herself down and penned the following immortal lines:

"There was no possibility of taking a walk that day. We had been wandering, indeed, in the leafless shrubbery an hour in the morning; but since dinner (Mrs Reed, when there was no company, dined early) the cold winter wind had brought with it clouds so sombre and a rain so penetrating, that further outdoor exercise was now out of the question."

It was the first paragraph of the first chapter of "Jane Eyre."

☆　　☆ ☆　　☆

Nobody wanted Charlotte's first novel, "The Professor", at least until her reputation had been secured with her three later novels and then not till 1857, when it was published posthumously. In spite of obvious faults in character and construction it is neverthelesss very readable, if only as a fore-runner to "Villette" which deals much more successfully with the same theme, i.e., Charlotte's stay in the Pensionnat Heger in Brussels.

Whilst she was still engaged in the writing of "Jane Eyre" her sisters, Emily and Anne, struck lucky (on the face of it) by having "Wuthering Heights" and "Agnes Grey" accepted by T.C. Newby (of 172 Mortimer Street, Cavendish Square) 'on terms somewhat impoverishing to the two authors.' They were first asked to contribute £50 towards the cost of printing and publication. The two novels were then held in abeyance for some months and, in fact, were not published until December 1847, two months after the appearance of "Jane Eyre."

On August 24th of that year Charlotte despatched by rail to Messrs Smith, Elder at 65 Cornhill "a MS entitled "Jane Eyre", a novel in three volumes, by Currer Bell." They had previously rejected "The Professor", but in very courteous and considerate terms, adding a rider that they would be prepared to give attention to something more suitable.

The manuscript on receipt was passed to the firm's

reader, a Mr Williams, (with whom Charlotte was later to indulge in a voluminous correspondence). He was so struck with it that he passed it to a second reader, "a clear-headed Scotchman, not given to enthusiasm . . ." (who "became so deeply interested in it, as to sit up half the night to finish it"). In turn it was passed to Mr Smith himself who partook of sandwiches in lieu of dinner so as to waste no time over its perusal. He endorsed everything both his readers had said about it.

"Jane Eyre" was published on 16th October 1847, less than two months after its receipt. It was almost immediately a best-seller. 'Currer Bell' its anonymous author became quite literally the talk of the town.

Only then did T.C. Newby proceed with the publication of "Wuthering Heights" and "Agnes Grey". He had good reason to, as will soon become apparent.

☆   ☆ ☆   ☆

Chapter 29

INTERLUDE – LONDON (July 1848)

ON THE EVENING of Friday, 7th July 1848, Charlotte, accompanied by her sister Anne, walked the four miles to Keighley (in a thunderstorm) and from there caught the connecting train to Leeds and the night train to London. They paid £2.5.6d each for First Class tickets and did not grudge the unaccustomed expense. It ensured them privacy. Also, by now, they felt they were in a position to afford it.

Charlott's intention was to pay a surprise call on her publisher, Smith, Elder at 65 Cornhill. It was a journey undertaken only as a matter of vital necessity.

In a letter to her former Roe Head school friend, Mary Taylor, who had since emigrated to New Zealand, she gave some details of the circumstances which had prompted her sudden decision. "One morning, at the beginning of July, a communication was received at the Parsonage from Messrs Smith and Elder, which disturbed its quiet inmates not a little ... 'Jane Eyre' had had a great run in America, and a publisher there had consequently bid high for early sheets of the next work by 'Currer Bell.' These Messrs Smith and Elder had promised to let him have. He was therefore greatly astonished, and not well pleased, to learn that a similar agreement had been entered into with another American house, and that the new tale was very shortly to appear. It turned out, upon inquiry, that the mistake had originated in Acton and Ellis Bell's publisher having assured this American house that, to the best of his belief, 'Jane Eyre,' 'Wuthering Heights,' and 'The Tenant of Wildfell Hall' (which he pronounced superior to either of the other two) were all written by the same author."

Mr J.C. Newby of Mortimer Street who (after some months of delay) had promptly published 'Wuthering

144

Heights' and 'Agnes Grey' consequent upon the wave of success that had floated (and continued to float) 'Jane Eyre' was undoubtedly all too willing to believe that the three and distinctly individual writers were but one. To that end also he almost fell over himself to rush Anne's second novel 'The Tenant of Wildfell Hall' into print in June 1848. The sisters were convinced that it was he who was now dabbling in the American market and had got them into comparatively hot water with Smith, Elder.

Newby, of course, was not the only one to persist in thinking that all four novels were the product of a single author. Many reviewers of the time were of the same opinion, in particular those who were inclined to find their subject matter and treatment not altogether in the best of taste. 'Jane Eyre' was either damned with faint praise or openly execrated (as in the case of Miss Rigby of the Quarterly Review of December 1848 who remarked of the author that 'She must be one who for some sufficient reason has long forfeited the society of her sex'). Only the critic of The Examiner would appear to have been un-qualified in his praise.

'Wuthering Heights' and 'The Tenant of Wildfell Hall' were both condemned in no uncertain fashion, it being felt there was 'something nasty in the woodshed' on both properties. The inclination, perhaps naturally, was to assign all that was considered 'scandalous' and 'unseemly' in the novels to the work of one hand. The Dublin Magazine openly stated so, to which Charlotte (in a letter to Mr Williams, the reader employed by Smith, Elder) retorted — "an ingenious thought in the reviewer, — very original and striking, but not accurate. We are three."

Only 'Agnes Grey' escaped any stern censure, being considered almost innocuous, in fact. It was all the more astounding that the same author could have dealt so frankly with the subject of drunkenness and profligacy in 'The Tenant of Wildfell Hall'. Even Charlotte was shaken by it and had to resort to making excuses for her sister in a later edition, calling as she did Branwell's unbridled behaviour to mind.

The fact remains that in spite of the critics the reading

public (hungry, as ever, for sensation) rushed to buy the so-called 'naughty' novels. J.C. Newby was to be excused for wanting to cash in on their resulting notoriety.

☆   ☆ ☆   ☆

Charlotte and Anne arrived in London early on Saturday morning. For Charlotte it was a renewal of old acquaintance. For Anne it was an entirely new and somewhat bewildering experience.

Before presenting themselves at the offices of Smith, Elder they obviously needed a wash and brush up of sorts (after their smoky journey) and something in the way of breakfast. Charlotte was aware of only one place that would serve both these needs, the obligatory Chapter Coffee House in Paternoster Row where she had previously stayed with her father and her sister Emily preparatory to proceeding to Ostend and Brussels.

Mrs Gaskell says that when planning their excursion to London, the day before, "they had resolved to take a cab, if they should find it desirable, from their inn to Cornhill; but amidst the bustle and 'queer state of inward excitement' in which they found themselves, as they sat and considered their position on the Saturday morning, they quite forgot even the possibility of hiring a conveyance; and when they set forth, they became so dismayed by the crowded streets, and the impeded crossings, that they stood still repeatedly, in complete despair of making progress, and were nearly an hour in walking the half-mile they had to go."

Nobody at 65 Cornhill had any idea they were coming. There had been no time for such niceties anyway. On receipt of the firm's letter of complaint Charlotte and Anne had literally taken off on the spot. They were not prepared to defend their reputation by mail. As for Emily, the matter would appear to have given her no concern whatever. She was prepared to leave Haworth for nothing and nobody.

The two sisters had not even bothered to ascertain whether or not the publishing and bookseller's business of

Smith, Elder was open on a Saturday morning. Even in those days it was quite customary for some city firms to decamp en bloc for the long weekend. As luck would have it, however, there were several clerks and assistants hanging about in the ground floor shop and of one of them Charlotte enquired if they might be ushered into the presence of Mr George Smith who (though still a young man) was then the nominal head of the firm.

Only their obvious determination gained the two sisters admission to the great man's inner sanctum and it must indeed have shaken him from his customary calm to be suddenly confronted with two rather plain little spinster ladies dressed in as plain and old-fashioned clothes. When Charlotte laid before him the very same letter he had addressed to 'Currer Bell' at Haworth Parsonage only a couple of days previously he was even more astounded. "Where did you get this?" he gasped.

Charlotte could only tell him how and why and for what reason they had come. In that surprising way she introduced herself as the author of 'Jane Eyre', his particular bright star, his best-selling novelist of the season, or, (if it comes to that) any other season he could recall.

☆　　☆ ☆　　　☆

It says much for the character of young George Smith, (he was only 24 at the time of first meeting Charlotte), that he could not do enough to make the two sister's short stay in London agreeable. Once having assured himself that there was no duplicity on their part in the matter of the American publication of 'The Tenant of Wildfell Hall' he insisted on showing them off to his literary friends and relations. On her part, however, Charlotte wished, as far as possible, that the 'Bell's' (as distinct from the 'Bronte's') should retain their anonymity. In this she was prompted to respect her sister Emily's feelings as much (if not more) than her own.

Nevertheless, that same evening, the two 'famous authors' were called on by him (at the Chapter Coffee House) and whirled off to the Opera House in Covent

Garden where they saw a performance of "The Barber of Seville" which Charlotte later described as "very brilliant, though I fancy there are things I should like better." The occasion was marred for them, however, by the fact that (as Mrs Gaskell states) "they had no fine elegant dresses either with them, or in the world" and in consequence felt decidedly out of place among the more fashionably dressed members of London Society.

The following day, Sunday, they attended morning service at St. Stephen's, Walbrook in company with Smith, Elder's Chief Reader, Mr Williams. That same afternoon 'Mr Smith and his mother fetched us in a carriage, and took us to his house to dine.'

Mr Smith's house was then in Westbourne Place (near Paddington Station). The whole area has since been 'developed' out of all recognition, as I sadly discovered when I went looking for the 'green-grocer's shop' which I was given to understand had for some time occupied part of the actual building (as a butcher's shop still forms part of Charlotte's birthplace in Thornton). I was pleased to note, however, that nearby Gloucester Terrace (to which the Smith family later moved) still, mercifully, remains intact.

George Smith himself was a quite remarkable figure in the publishing world. He was responsible for publishing not only the works of Charlotte Bronte but also included in his list of authors such illustrious names as Thackeray, Robert Browning, and Matthew Arnold. In 1865 (in conjunction with Frederick Greenwood) he founded 'The Pall Mall Gazette' and in 1882 was both founder and proprietor of the 'Dictionary of National Biography' which still prominently features on reference library shelves.

Charlotte and Anne were kept more or less in non-stop flight until they arrived back at Haworth on Tuesday, the 11th July, having paid (obligatory) visits to the Royal Academy and the National Gallery, dined again at Mr Smith's and taken tea with Mr Williams.

In between, Charlotte (in her own words) had suffered "a racking headache and harassing sickness . . ." From the peace and quiet of the Parsonage she reflects – "A more jaded wretch than I looked, it would be difficult to conceive. I was thin when I went, but I was meagre indeed when I returned . . . In a while, however, these bad effects of excitement went off, and I regained my normal condition."

Anne would appear to have worn much better, though we have no corresponding comment from her on the experience. Emily was no doubt amused by what they had to tell. Otherwise, she was completely indifferent.

☆　　　☆ ☆　　　　☆

Chapter 30

HAWORTH (July 1848 - May 1849)

WE HAVE BEEN given to understand that poor Branwell knew nothing of what was going on at this time vis-a-vis his sisters and their publishers and the world at large. I find this very hard to believe, unless Branwell was non compos mentis for twenty-four hours out of twenty-four.

Indeed in July 1848 he was sufficiently aware of what was going on around him to intreat help from his friend Joseph Leyland (of Luddenden Foot days) in the matter of an outstanding debt which the landlord of the Old Cock Inn at Halifax had threatened (in a letter to Mr Bronte) to take legal proceedings over. His endeavours to extricate himself from this particularly awkward situation (and others of a like kind), though proving him to be quite distraught, show no evidence of a mental incapacity to override his difficulties.

Given that he occasionally had lucid moments it seems inconceivable that he should not have questioned the inordinate amount of mail the postman was delivering to the Parsonage (including frequent parcels of gift books bestowed on Charlotte by Smith, Elder through their reader, Mr Williams). Were those books (including those which the sisters themselves had published) so secreted about the house that he was at no time aware of their existence? If they were so hidden away from him, does it not reflect something not a little underhand in the girls' dealings with their unfortunate brother?

In a famous passage from Mrs Gaskell's 'Life of Charlotte Bronte' Charlotte is portrayed as informing her father that she has "been writing a book" only after she is able to put a printed copy in his hands, together with some of the more favourable reviews of 'Jane Eyre'. He seems to have supposed at first that it was in manuscript and to have queried the expense she might be put to in getting it printed. His surprise seems almost naive when, on coming into tea after reading it, he remarks to the assembled company, (Branwell being conveniently absent, of course), "Girls, do you know Charlotte has been writing a book, and it is much better than likely?"

He must obviously have been aware that all the children had been 'writing books' since their early childhood. Was he not also aware that they had previously published a collection of poems, though at a loss and at their own expense? It would almost appear that he had been divorced completely from his daughters' confidence as regards their literary aims and aspirations . . .

Not credible, surely. Their father, too, had published poems and stories of a kind. One would suppose that they would be the more keen on that account to acquaint him with their own plans to print and publish what they had obviously been engaged on for some months past. Or did they feel that his rather feeble efforts would not stand just comparison with their own? Was it for that reason that poor Branwell was entirely excluded from any part in it, who had so eagerly collaborated with them in the production of the 'little magazines' with their interminable poems, plays, and stories? Was he to be told nothing of the phenomenal success of 'Jane Eyre'? Was he to be kept in complete ignorance of the publication of 'Wuthering Heights', 'Agnes Grey', and 'The Tenant of Wildfell Hall' (all of which were on sale to the general public before his untimely death in the autumn of 1848)?

Could he possibly have been unaware of the little volume of poems in which his sisters had collaborated and which he had not been invited to contribute to? Ambitious as he was in that direction, why had he been so pointedly passed over?

It would seem that not enough has been said on this matter.

☆ ☆ ☆ ☆

All through that summer of 1848 Branwell's condition

deteriorated. So long as he had money (and he took the most extraordinary measures to obtain it) he was, quite literally, able to keep up his dwindling supply of spirits . . . At the druggist's shop (opposite the Bull Hotel) he more and more frequently obtained his little squib of laundanum, either by purchase, (or, when his credit ran out, pleading for sheer pity's sake that he might be put out of his misery at no further cost to himself). It was inevitable that he should thus hasten his death. There was nothing more left to him to achieve.

His railway engineer friend from Halifax, Francis Grundy, said later that he dined with him over a couple of glasses of hot brandy in the Black Bull only a few days before he died. His head, appearing round the door, "was a mass of red unkempt uncut hair, wildly floating round a great gaunt forehead; the cheeks yellow and hollow, the mouth fallen, the thin lips not trembling but shaking, the sunken eyes, once small now glaring with the light of madness . . . He described himself as waiting anxiously for death — indeed, longing for it, and happy, in these sane moments, to think that it was so near. He once again declared that that death would be due to the story I knew, and to nothing else . . ."

Grundy meant, of course, the story of his tragic liaison with Mrs Robinson, but I can't help wondering if there was more to it than that. Did he not feel himself to have been completely abandoned by his family during those last few months? And if, in fact, he knew of his sisters' success and thought they were hiding it from him would he not, as a consequence, have become more and more bitter — more obsessed with the utter hopelessness of his position?

It has been suggested that he had a hand in the making of 'Wuthering Heights' and (possibly) 'The Tenant of Wildfell Hall'. There is nothing to substantiate this, though who was in a better position to supply the material background for the scenes of violence in both novels? On the other hand, it must be said that he was quite incapable of the sustained effort necessary to their completion.

The cause of his death (on Sunday morning, 24th September) was certified as "Chronic bronchis-marasmus" (a wasting away of the body tissues). Simply, he died from complete exhaustion of all his faculties.

Writing to Ellen Nussey, a fortnight later, Charlotte reflected that "the spectacle of his pale corpse gave me more acute pain than I could have imagined. Till the last hour comes, we never know how much we can forgive, pity, regret a near relative. All his vices were and are nothing now. We remember only his woes . . ."

Poor Mr Bronte remembered much more than that. He remembered the death of his wife and the death of their first-born infants, little Maria and Elizabeth. He recalled young Branwell's brilliant childhood and the promise he had shown which was never fulfilled. "My poor father naturally thought more of his *only* son than of his daughters," Charlotte wrote later to Mr Williams, "and much and long as he had suffered on his account, he cried out for his loss like David for that of Absalom — my son! — my son!"

He must have wondered why the God to whom he had dedicated his life should continue to scourge him so unmercifully. He was not to know that from now on he was to continue to reel from those whip lashes; that what he had suffered before was as nothing to what he was to be compelled to suffer in the months ahead.

☆   ☆ ☆   ☆

The wicket gate between the church and the Parsonage was again opened on Thursday, 28th September, and Branwell's body was borne through it for the last time. He had never been a frequent visitor there, the last two occasions being on the burial of his friend Willie Weightman and his aunt, Elizabeth Branwell. He is said to have expired with the whispered word "Amen" on his lips. It was his final concession to the Christian God who may be saddled with having dealt so unfairly with him. Was that a last bitterly-wrung comment on his wasted life, or a sign of submission to the will of his Creator and a hope for absolution to come?

His sister Emily, who at all times was closest to him in

spirit, had been the one member of the family (apart from their poor father) willing to extend to him her full sympathy and understanding. On her had fallen the task (on so many occasions) of seeking him out in the Black Bull and other local taverns and literally hauling him upstairs to bed. Her reward was to be stricken with a cold at his funeral, a cold from which she was never to recover.

The progress of her illness is best described in Charlotte's recorded correspondence at that time. On 29th October, 1848, she writes, "Emily's cold and cough are very obstinate ... She looks very thin and pale. Her reserved nature occasions me great uneasiness of mind. It is useless to question her; you get no answers. It is still more useless to recommend remedies; they are never adopted."

On November 23rd Emily is *"very* ill ... Her pulse, the only time she allowed it to be felt, was found to beat 115 per minute. In this state she resolutely refuses to see a doctor ..."

On the very morning that she lay dying, Charlotte (maybe sitting at her bedside) wrote that she was daily growing weaker. "The physician's opinion" (Emily had grudgingly permitted one to be sent for)" was expressed too obscurely to be of use. He sent some medicine, which she would not take ..."

It was too late, anyway. Emily, still resolutely refusing to die in bed (or to die at all, if it comes to that) drew her last gasp on the dining room sofa, her eyes too dim to discern the sprig of heather which Charlotte had but lately fetched from her beloved moors. "No coward soul is mine ..." she had written, as part of the enduring legend she left to posterity. It was two o'clock in the afternoon of Tuesday the 19th of December, 1848. She had gone to whatever heaven it was she believed in, a little less than three months after Branwell had departed for his. The time lapse was not much longer than that which intervened between the deaths of her sister Maria and her sister Elizabeth.

"Emily suffers no more from pain or weakness now," wrote Charlotte, two days after. "she never will suffer more in this world. She is gone, after a hard, short conflict . . . No need now to tremble for the hard frost and the keen wind. Emily does not feel them. She died in a time of promise . . ."

Not least among the mourners at her funeral was her faithful old bulldog, Keeper. That same dog she had beaten unmercifully with her bare hands after he had dared to stretch himself luxuriously on one of the upstair counterpanes came home with the stricken father and his two remaining children, lay down at Emily's own door, and howled pitifully for many days. Charlotte's account of her sister's passing may well be the most poignant thing she ever wrote. Keeper's comment was the more apt as one who vainly tried to speak for all the dumb animals she had made it her business to speak up for. She was their voice who had served her better than any human being she had cared to know.

☆   ☆ ☆   ☆

A few short weeks after Branwell died his faithless mistress, Lydia Robinson, married Sir Edward Dolman Scott. In as little time after Emily died her beloved sister Anne was herself making preparations to join the three people she had most cared for in her short life; her brother, her sister, and Willie Weightman.

She had never been strong and now she visibly weakened from day to day. On January 10th, 1849, Charlotte wrote to Ellen Nussey: "Anne had a very tolerable day yesterday, and a pretty quiet night last night, though she did not sleep much . . . She looks somewhat pale and sickly. She has had one dose of the cod-liver oil; it smells and tastes like train oil . . ." Five days later she reports her sister as not being any worse, nor any better. "The morning is usually the best time;" (she says) "the afternoon and the evening the most feverish. Her cough is the most troublesome at nights . . ."

On March 24th she describes Anne's decline as "gradual and fluctuateing." In spirit, she seemed resigned; at heart, a true Christian. "May God support her" (she says) "and all of us through the trial of lingering sickness, and aid her in the last hour, when the struggle which separates soul from body must be gone through . . ." It would seem that she had already resigned herself to losing another sister to that same dread complaint, Consumption, which had regularly stalked her family in the past. But unlike Emily who "Never in all her life" had "lingered over any task that lay before her," who "sank rapidly", who "made haste to leave us . . ." Anne was to linger well into the Spring and to choose another place than Haworth and her native West Riding in which to resign herself to the inevitable.

Resignation came as naturally to Anne as rebellion to Branwell and Emily. It was submission to the whims of fate that had kept her nose to the domestic grindstone far longer and more consistently than any other of her restless family, with the possible exception of Mr Bronte himself.

☆   ☆ ☆   ☆

Chapter 31

INTERLUDE – SCARBOROUGH (May 1849)

I HAVE MANY happy memories of Scarborough which, not without reason, has been called 'The Queen of Watering Places.' Its two fabulous bays (North and South) are distinct from each other in catering for those who want only peace and quiet and those who prefer to be constantly entertained and amused. Its scenery is incomparable.

I recall autumnal cliff-top walks and untenanted stretches of sand; its boisterous and colourful harbour (in mid-August) crowded with fishing smacks and well-patronised cockle and whelk stalls; an evening's entertainment at the Open Air Theatre in Northstead Manor Gardens with the Black & White Minstrels in strident chorus; the droll buffoonery of Frankie Howerd and the almost continuous strains of Max Jaffa and his Orchestra (so long an integral part of the summer season). Only recently I read that he was still entertaining his fans with those occasional flashes of wit that bid fair to be recorded; as, for instance, that he now proposed to play a version of Handel's celebrated 'Water Music', as arranged by Denis Howell (the newly-appointed Minister for Drought).

Above all, and overlooking both Bays, stands what still remains of the town's ancient castle after its shelling by German submarines in the first World War. Ellen Nussey (Charlotte Bronte's friend) described it as standing "in proud glory gilded by the rays of the declining sun. The distant ships glittered like burnished gold; the little boats near the beach heaved on the ebbing tide, inviting occupants. The view was grand beyond description . . ."

It still looks pretty much the same today.

☆ ☆ ☆ ☆

Anne Bronte loved Scarborough, though it was a far less hectic place when she paid her annual visits there as governess to the Robinson family. In her mind's eye she was courted there (on the green slopes of Castle Hill) by Willie Weightman, her father's curate, and perforce had to rest content with transferring her vision to the final pages of 'Agnes Grey'.

It was from Scarborough that her brother received his marching orders from Lydia Robinson's outraged husband. It was to Scarborough that Anne returned . . . to die. By the far wall in St. Mary's Churchyard, at the foot of the Castle, she was laid to rest for ever; the only one of her family not to be buried under the cold flag-stones of St. Michael's Church in Haworth.

It was fitting, perhaps, for one whose devotion to duty had always demanded of her that she should be the longest away from home.

As she wrote in her last poem (January 1849) and most aptly, under the circumstances:

"I hoped amid the brave and strong
My portioned task might lie;
To toil amid the labouring throng
With purpose keen and high;
But Thou hast fixed another part . . ."

And (in a later verse from the same poem):

"That secret labour to sustain
With humble patience every blow;
To gather fortitude from pain,
And hope and holiness from woe."

Unlike her sister, Emily, she lingered long over every task and dealt the same with the business of dying. Charlotte reports, at various times through the early months of 1849 that she seemed "to be a little better during some mild days last week . . ." that "perhaps the return of really warm weather may give nature a happy stimulus . . ." that "there have been changes of temperature whose effect Anne has felt unfavourably" . . ."

The fact remains that Mr Bronte had been told by the doctor he summoned to attend his daughter (as early as the beginning of that year) that, in fact, there was no hope for her. The disease (consumption) had advanced so far that both lungs were badly affected. All that could be done was by way of alleviation of her sufferings. The fatal day was not to be put off indefinitely.

☆   ☆ ☆   ☆

It was Anne's most ardent wish that she might be given the opportunity to 'recuperate' in Scarborough and her own doctor agreed that it might well suit her to do so. But, not yet ... not yet ... was the constantly recurring theme. Always there was the hope that the weather would improve sufficient for her to undertake the journey and still it remained too changeable for the risk to be contemplated. As late as the beginning of May, while arrangements were being made for her removal to the seaside, Charlotte was writing to Ellen (who was to accompany them both there) "I wish my judgment sanctioned the step of going to Scarborough more fully than it does ..."

It was not until the end of that month that it was finally decided the trip should be made. Rooms had been booked at No. 2, The Cliff, an extensive (and expensive) boarding house consisting of several suites of separate lodgings (on St. Nicholas Cliff, overlooking the South Bay). This establishment (whose site is now completely covered by the Grand Hotel) was known as "Wood's Lodgings" and much favoured by summer visitors to the town. The Robinson family had themselves made a point of staying there and this, no doubt, influenced Anne's choice of it. She had recently been left some money in the will of an old Thornton friend of the family who, learning of the girl's illness, (whilst on her own death bed), thought it might help in paving the way to her recovery. Expense was therefore no immediate object. Indeed, Anne no doubt derived a certain wry satisfaction from the thought of returning as a guest to the place where she had once served as a governess.

It had been arranged that Ellen Nussey should meet the two sisters at Leeds station on Wednesday, May 23rd, but (unknown to her) Anne had suffered a relapse that same morning and in consequence the appointment could not be kept. Ellen watched train after train come in, from two of which coffins had been carried to waiting hearses. Tired of waiting, she eventually decided to return home and present herself at the Parsonage on the following morning.

As luck would have it she arrived at the side gate just in time to see Charlotte and Anne emerge from the house, followed by Mr Bronte and Martha Brown (the sexton's daughter and long a good and faithful servant to the Bronte family). A chaise was waiting there and the invalid, still very feeble, was lifted into it. Martha said she saw Death written on that face, but Charlotte (equally aware of it) made no comment. She turned and waved to her father and his helpmate (no doubt the two dogs, Flossy and Keeper, were gazing as pathetically after them) and the chaise moved off in the direction of Keighley. It was Anne's last glimpse of her old home.

The first stage of their journey on that 24th day of May ended at York. They had dinner in the George Hotel in Coney Street (from which ran the coaches to Scarborough) and then decided to pay a visit to the famous Minster. Anne had been there before, when working for the Robinson family and again with Emily on her return from Thorp Green. The revival of so many happy memories cheered her immensely. "If finite power can do this, what is the . . .?" she whispered to Charlotte and Ellen. Emotion would not allow her to continue her train of thought.

They did a little shopping whilst in the city, spending more than they normally would have contemplated on bonnets and other feminine fancies, a necessary prelude to visiting such a fashionable seaside resort. They then returned to the George Hotel for a night's rest before continuing their journey by rail to Scarborough on the following day.

Anne sat by her bedroom window looking out on the sea for most of the remainder of that day. "She says if she could breathe more freely she would be comfortable," wrote Charlotte later, to Mr Williams, — "but she cannot breathe freely." Ellen Nussey too remarked of her condition at that time, "After such an exertion as walking to her bedroom, she would clasp her hands and raise her eyes in silent thanks, and she did this not to the exclusion of wonted prayer, for that too was performed on bended knee, ere she accepted the rest of her couch."

On the following day (Saturday) she insisted on driving in a donkey-carriage along the smooth stretch of sand where the tide had gone out and is said to have taken to task the boy in charge of the conveyance for urging the poor beast to greater speed. Like Emily, she was ever watchful that no harm should come to the dumb animals we use for our convenience. It would have horrified her to see what heavy loads some of these small creatures are called upon to bear in the shape of overweight ed holiday-makers on the sands of some of our modern seaside resorts.

The following morning (Sunday) she wanted to go to church but Charlotte, with some difficulty, dissuaded her. Instead she agreed to walk out a little way with them in the afternoon and having done so begged to be left on her own for awhile to sit on a bench overlooking the sea where she might enjoy the view with no distraction.

That same evening she watched the sun go down over the castle from an easy chair drawn up close to her window. She too was sinking fast, but at that time gave no visible sign of it, absorbed as she was in her private thoughts. The following morning (in the words of Ellen Nussey) "She rose at seven o'clock, and performed most of her toilet herself, by her expressed wish ... Nothing occurred to excite alarm till about 11 a.m. She then spoke of feeling a change. 'She believed she had not long to live. Could she reach home alive, if we prepared immediately for departure?' A physician was sent for (who) ... reluctantly admitted that the angel of death was already arrived, and that life was ebbing fast ..."

Like her sister Emily (less than six months before) "she was borne to the sofa ..." There she "calmly and without a sigh passed from the temporal to the eternal ..." Her last words (and clearly spoken) were for her sister. "Take courage, Charlotte, take courage!"

The time was around two o'clock on Monday afternoon, the 28th May. "So little was the house disturbed by the presence of the dying, and the sorrow of those so nearly bereaved" (wrote Ellen) "that dinner was announced as ready through the half-open door, as the living sister was closing the eyes of the dead."

They laid her quietly to rest in St. Mary's Churchyard two days later. She was not yet thirty years old. Emily had just turned that age. Branwell was but a year older.

In the short space of eight months the stricken father had been bereft of three out of four of his remaining children. He might well have wondered what he had done to be again and again visited by the implacable Reaper of his small field.

☆   ☆ ☆   ☆

Chapter 32

HAWORTH (June 1849 - March 1855)

MR BRONTE DID not attend the funeral of his youngest child. Charlotte thought it was too much to expect of him, just as she had no wish that he should be dragged through another harrowing burial service at Haworth. It was for that reason they left Anne where she most wanted to be.

At her father's insistence Charlotte (in company with Ellen) spent another three weeks by the sea; first at Filey and later with the Hudson family near Bridlington where she and Ellen had previously stayed in the autumn of 1839. She returned to Haworth on 21st June.

"I got here a little before eight o'clock," she said later, in a letter to Ellen. "All was clean and bright waiting for me. Papa and the servants were well; and all received me with an affection which should have consoled. The dogs seemed in strange ecstasy. I am certain they regarded me as the harbinger of others. The dumb creatures thought that as I was returned, those who had been so long absent were not far behind . . ."

Nothing could more poignantly have described her lonely situation.

As some form of antidote she busied herself with the writing of "Shirley" which she had begun almost immediately after the publication of "Jane Eyre". That it turned out to be her least successful novel is due mainly to the fact that, of necessity, it was never pursued consistently but only in a series of fits and starts. It would be an understatement, indeed, to say that Charlotte had too much else on her mind at the time.

Nevertheless, when finally published by Smith, Elder in October of that year it was quite favourably reviewed by the critics (albeit with a scarcely veiled feeling of disappointment that it contained nothing that could justly be called 'scandalous' and which had contributed so much to the success of "Jane Eyre." Like the curate's egg, however, it was good in parts, especially the lambasting of her father's curates in the opening chapter which caused a great deal of laughter and a certain amount of acid comment from those most likely to be affected by it. But, in general, its setting (in the West Riding) pleased both those who were well acquainted with the locality and those whose knowledge of it stopped short at Oxford. Charlotte wrote nothing better than her account of the attack on Rawfolds Mill by the Luddites in Chapter XIX ("A Summer Night"). She wrote nothing worse, certainly nothing more tedious and boring, than Chapter XXVII of the same novel ("The First Blue-Stocking").

One result of the success of "Shirley" was to make widely known the real name of its author. People in the immediate neighbourhood could not fail to recognise the true characters depicted therein as distinct from their fictional representation. As Mrs Gaskell remarks, "'Airedale, Wharfdale, Calderdale, and Ribblesdale' all knew the place of residence of Currer Bell . . . All round about the news had spread; strangers came 'from beyond Burnley' to see her, as she went quietly and unconsciously into church; and the sexton 'gained many a half-crown' for pointing her out."

'Currer Bell' was dead, and Charlotte Bronte could at last openly claim credit for the impact she had made on the reading public. There was no reason now why it should be otherwise. Poor Emily was no longer there to voice her disapproval of the resulting publicity.

Indeed, she would no doubt have been horrified at the change this brought about in Charlotte's circumstances. She was now able to drop the cloak of anonymity that had shrouded her true identity and appear (quite frequently) in London Society as the author of "Jane Eyre". Over the next few years she was assiduously courted by lords and ladies and the literary celebrities of the time, including Thackeray and Harriet Martineau (that 'ardent advocate of social reform' and defender of 'Woman's Rights'). She wined and dined and stayed in the houses of those who far excelled in affluence and distinction any she had once been called upon the serve in a humble (and sometimes degrading) capacity. Those who had once treated her with indifference, if not contempt, now saw her elevated to a position they could never hope to attain. Poor Branwell would have loved nothing better than to change places with her. It had always been his ambition to walk on terms of equality with the greatest and most illustrious of his time.

Yet, through it all, Charlotte remained her true self — the daughter of a comparative obscure parson in a comparatively obscure Yorkshire village. Though she travelled more extensively than she had ever done before and that in response to the many pressing demands she received, it was to Haworth that she always returned (and that most thankfully). It was the only place where she was not visited with nervous exhaustion and constantly recurring sick headaches.

Mrs Gaskell relates, graphically, that "owing to Mr Bronte's great age", (he was then well over 70), "and long-formed habits of solitary occupation when in the house, his daughter was left to herself for the greater part of the day . . . The hours of retiring for the night had always been early in the Parsonage; now family prayers were at eight o'clock; directly after which Mr Bronte and old Tabby went to bed, and Martha was not long in following. But Charlotte could not have slept if she had gone, — could not have rested on her desolate couch. She stopped up, — it was very tempting, — late and later; striving to beguile the lonely night with some employment, till her weak eyes failed to read or to sew, and could only weep in solitude over the dead that were not. No one on earth can even imagine what those hours were to her . . ."

Every so often she would be off again somewhere, not because she was enamoured of company but because it offered her some temporary relief. She went (on several occasions) to London, to the Lake District, even as far as Edinburgh, which she compared to London as being "like a vivid page of history compared to a large dull treatise on political economy." She indulged in voluminous correspondence with her publisher's reader, Mr Williams, and some of the leading critics of the day, including George Lewes and Miss Martineau. She sturdily defended her own writings and those of her dead sisters and was not above criticising other peoples (including those of her particular hero, · William Makepeace Thackeray). But at heart she remained the lonely, independant creature she had always been, most proud of her father's simple admiration and that of her own domestic servants. "Martha came in yesterday, puffing and blowing, and much excited." (she wrote to Ellen in February 1850). ' "I've heard such news,' she began. 'What about?' 'Please ma'am, you've been and written two books, the grandest books that ever was seen . . .' "

Fame she had and a certain amount of the independance that goes with it (she had received £500 each for 'Jane Eyre' and 'Shirley' and had begun the writing of 'Villette', her last completed novel) but she was still most her natural self in the domestic atmosphere of her home on the moors with all the memories of the past it conjured up. Her concern for the future was still bound up with the responsibility she felt she owed to her aging father and his long-serving and faithful dependants.

☆   ☆ ☆   ☆

All her life Charlotte had had an inferiority complex with regard to her personal appearance. Mrs Gaskell (as previously mentioned) described her features as "plain, large, and ill-set" and went on relentlessly to refer to her "crooked mouth" and her "large nose". Mary Taylor (at Roe Head) saw her first as "a little old woman, so short-sighted that she always appeared to be seeking something, and moving her head from side to side to catch sight of it." George Smith, her publisher, in an article in the Cornhill Magazine (December 1900) said "There was but little feminine charm about her . . ." and that she was all too conscious of the fact herself. He believed she would have given all her genius and all her fame to have been beautiful. Nevertheless, at one time, his name was linked with hers as a possible suitor and we know for a fact that she received a proposal from James Taylor (Smith, Elder's business manager) and turned him down because (as she told Ellen Nussey) " . . . each moment he came near me, and that I could see his eyes fastened on me my veins ran ice."

She had similarly turned down a proposal from Henry Nussey (Ellen's brother) because she "could not have that intense attachment" (towards him) "which would make me willing to die for him; and, if ever I marry, it must be in that light of adoration that I will regard my husband . . ." Not that she had any intention of marrying. "I am certainly doomed to be an old maid," (she told Ellen). "Never mind, I made up my mind to that fate ever since I was twelve years old . . ."

Life (as distinct from her romantic notions about it) was to give the lie to both statements in a very short time. She was indeed to marry and whatever other feelings she might have for her future husband it was most certainly not in the "light of adoration" that she was to regard him.

☆   ☆ ☆   ☆

Arthur Bell Nicholls (an Ulsterman of Scottish ancestry) first came to Haworth in May 1845 as curate to Mr Bronte. He proved to be able and efficient but was not altogether popular (mainly on account of his rather cold disposition and strictly sectarian views). Certainly he was the complete antithesis of the late sadly lamented Willie Weightman.

From the start he appears to have made little, if any, impression on Charlotte. She mentions him in passing (writing to Ellen on 10th July, 1846) when some local gossip had hinted at their possible marriage. "I scarcely need say that never was rumour more unfounded. A cold far-away sort of civility are the only terms on which I have ever been with Mr Nicholls."

On his part, however, the same could not be said though he appears to have been content to admire her from a distance. Admire her, he did. He arrived on the scene in time to see how she coped with the disgrace brought on the family by her erring brother and the threat to their livelihood entailed by Mr Bronte's failing health. He saw how bravely and uncomplainingly she faced up to the deaths, in quick succession, of those most near and dear to her. He was even more gratified to note that fame and comparative fortune had made little, if any, impression on her simple, strong-minded character. And from the silence on all these matters which he had so far maintained he began to indulge a faint hope . . .

One evening in December 1852 he took the bull by the horns. He had been to tea with Mr Bronte and his daughter and (as Charlotte remarks of the occasion) "I vaguely felt without clearly seeing, as without seeing I have felt for some time, the meaning of his constant looks, and strange, feverish restraint . . ." After tea he sat alone with Mr Bronte till between eight and nine o'clock. "I then heard him open the parlour door as if going," says Charlotte. "I expected the clash of the front door. He stopped in the passage; he tapped; like lightning it flashed upon me what was coming . . ."

What was coming, in fact, was a stammered, almost uncontrollable declaration of his love for her. Mr Nicholls had kept quiet for too long (for nearly eight years from the day he first saw her). It was not to be endured any longer. But when the flood-gates burst at last he went to pieces altogether. He became almost pathetic.

Mr Bronte certainly thought so and when Charlotte approached him on the matter (Mr Nicholls was too scared to do so) his reaction was most violent. He forebade his daughter to have any further dealings with so humble a suitor and confirmed his decision in a written note to the offending curate. He was of the opinion that Charlotte was now in a position to take her pick among the highest in the land. At his most snobbish stand-point he entirely overlooked his own humble beginnings.

Had Charlotte really been in love with Mr Nicholls (as she proved to have been in love with M. Heger in her novel 'Villette', published a month later) she would not have taken things quite so calmly. As it was, she allowed herself to be overruled by her father, preferring to let events take their natural course rather than impress her own personality upon them. She had chosen that way of life both for Jane Eyre and Lucy Snowe.

Mr Nicholls meanwhile found himself faced with an impossible situation and the only way out of it was to get out as soon as possible. On 27th March, 1853, he left Haworth (seemingly for good and all) having been offered a curacy at Kirk Smeaton, near Pontefract. The previous evening Charlotte found him literally in tears at the Parsonage gate. In attempting to console him she only made matters worse. She encouraged him to go on hoping . . .

He wrote her some half-a-dozen pleading letters before she deigned to acknowledge that (at least) she pitied his hopeless situation. From then on correspondence flowed between them. In January 1854 he paid a visit to friends at neighbouring Oxenhope and Charlotte committed herself to meeting him there. In consequence she began to impress on her father that if he continued to deny himself the help and comfort of his former curate's administrations at Haworth he was likely to end up in an even worse position than hers. The more so when he had chosen to saddle himself with a fool in the shape of his new curate, Mr de Renzi.

Mr Bronte finally acknowledged the wisdom of her remarks and capitulated to the extent of allowing them to meet openly. It was but a short step from there to his agreeing (though still somewhat grudgingly) first to their becoming engaged, then to their marriage.

"Mr Nicholls is a kind, considerate fellow." (wrote Charlotte to Ellen). "With all his masculine faults, he enters into my wishes about having the thing done quietly, in a way that makes me grateful . . ." Certainly the wedding, which took place at Haworth Parish Church on 29th June, 1854, could not have been much quieter. Mr Bronte himself cried off at the last moment and (having consulted the authority of the Prayer-book on the subject) deputized Miss Wooler, Charlotte's old school-mistress at Roe Head and Dewsbury, to give his daughter away. Apart from her, only Ellen Nussey was present (in the capacity of bridesmaid). None of Charlotte's new-found friends in the aristocratic and literary world turned up on this seemingly inauspicious occasion. They had not been informed or invited, anyway.

Let Mrs Gaskell have the last word on the subject:

"The news of the wedding had slipt abroad before the little party came out of the church, and many *old and humble* friends (my italics) were there, seeing her look 'like a snow-drop,' as they say. Her dress was white embroidered muslin, with a lace mantle, and white bonnet trimmed with green leaves, which perhaps might suggest the resemblance to the pale wintry flower."

☆   ☆ ☆   ☆

The happy couple (and there is no reason to suppose they were anything else) spent their honeymoon in Ireland, visiting Killarney, Tralee, Cork, and Dublin. In the latter city Charlotte was introduced to Mr Nicholls' cousin (with no inkling that she was later to become his second wife). They ended their tour at the family home in Banagher, Co. Offaly (King's County until the establishment of the Irish Free State in 1922). There is no record of their having visited any of Mr Bronte's Irish relations, which seems passing strange . . .

They returned to Haworth and (so far as Charlotte was concerned) to complete isolation. She had the joy of knowing that 'Villette' had proved as much a success as 'Jane Eyre' even though its 'scandalous' content had so far not linked her name with M. Heger in the sublimation of Lucy Snowe's abortive love affair with M. Paul Emanuel). There was *too much* love in the novel for Harriet Martineau's astringent taste but she was, luckily, unaware how truly it paralleled Charlotte's own personal experience. So was Arthur Bell Nicholls till much later when the knowledge could do him no harm.

His love was selfish enough not to want it shared by her literary friends and as a consequence she gave them up one by one and, if she did any writing at all, merely tinkered with it as time would allow. As she confided to Ellen,

" . . . the fact is, my time is not my own now; somebody else wants a good portion of it, and says 'we must do so and so.' We do so and so, accordingly; and it generally seems the right thing . . ." 'Poor Charlotte' . . . as Emily might well have commented could she have known.

Nevertheless, she would seem to have become resigned to life with Mr Nicholls, if not completely content. "I have a good, kind, attached husband;" (she said) "and every day my own attachment to him grows stronger." It was not exactly what she would have wished for Jane with Mr Rochester or Lucy with M. Emanuel but it served for Charlotte Bronte's own expectations.

And, after all, it was for so little a time. She had been comparatively immune from sick headaches for the first few months of married life but she could not avoid taking cold on the slightest occasion. It was bred in the bone, as could well be said of all her sisters. Walking out on her beloved moors with her not less beloved husband late in November she was caught in a sudden down-pour of rain. She never recovered from the chill it first engendered.

Indeed, she again caught cold early in the new year (1855) whilst visiting the home of an old friend and literary admirer, Sir James Kay Shuttleworth. This was occasioned by 'a long walk over damp ground in thin shoes . . .' As a consequence, on her return home, she took to her bed. There she begun the slow but relentless decline that had taken toll of Emily and Anne.

Her last two letters were written to her faithful friend, Ellen Nussey, and to an old acquaintance of her school-days in Brussels. To Ellen she confided the fact that in her husband she had found "the tenderest nurse, the kindest support, the best earthly comfort that ever woman had . . ." To Laetitia Wheelwright (late of the Rue d'Isabelle) she expressed much the same sentiments. "No kinder, better husband than mine, it seems to me, there can be in the world . . ."

Both letters were written in February, 1855. "About the third week in March" (says Mrs Gaskell) "there was a change; a low wandering delirium came on; and in it she begged constantly for food and even for stimulants. She swallowed eagerly now; but it was too late. Wakening for an instant from this stupor of intelligence, she saw her husband's woe-worn face, and caught the sound of some murmured words of prayer that God would spare her. 'Oh!' she whispered forth, 'I am not going to die, am I? He will not separate us, we have been so happy.' "

She died on Saturday morning, the 31st March. It was as though she had achieved all that God intended for her and it was much in the long run, far more than He had decreed for those who went before her. In marriage she had found the ultimate fulfilment; something denied to both her sisters and her only brother. She was one month short of her 39th birthday. That in itself was something to be thankful for. It was an extension of time He had not seen fit to allot to her beloved childhood companions.

The sublime irony was that in this final bereavement of her long-suffering father and the short-lived happiness of her chosen husband God saw fit to deprive them of the child in her womb who might yet have brought them some consolation. It might well be said that the history of the Bronte family was one of constant deprivation.

☆　　☆ ☆　　☆

EPILOGUE

MR BRONTE and Mr Nicholls returned to the empty Parsonage house after the funeral. Empty it was in every sense of the word, apart from the ghosts of the dear departed and the still cheerful ministrations of Martha Brown, their one remaining link with the reality of the domestic scene.

Poor old Tabitha Aykroyd (that most faithful of faithful servants) was no longer there to entertain (or irritate) them with recollections of 'the childer' who had so often plagued and pleased her in the past. She had died (in her 84th year) only six weeks before her beloved mistress. And well for her that she was spared this last of the family's many trials and troubles.

'Keeper' and 'Flossy' were themselves in whatever heaven we hope there is for dogs. Perhaps (who knows?) they had at last found what they had been seeking for so long . . .

The old man and his son-in-law had perforce to comfort each other as best they could. It was a labour of love for both of them, this mutual business of reconciling their differences, and sorely trying it must have been at times. Nevertheless they endured six long years of each other's company and found common ground in the administration of parochial affairs.

Mr Bronte died in 1861 at the age of 84, having long surrendered most of his ministerial duties to his younger and more capable helpmate. If, as has been suggested, Mr Nicholls was only concerned to step into his shoes and for that reason had passed up opportunities for promotion elsewhere, he was to be disappointed. The local elders who had first opposed Mr Bronte's right to election presented an even firmer front to the election of Mr Nicholls. They did not want him and they said so.

He elected to return to his native Ireland where (as

previously mentioned) he married his cousin. He had been husband to Charlotte for nine months only. His second marriage lasted for forty years, till his own death in 1906.

The wheel had turned full circle. From Ireland had come Patrick Bronte to have his name recorded indelibly on the roll-call of English history through the achievements of his remarkable daughters, Charlotte, Emily, and Anne. To Ireland his son-in-law returned, to be remembered likewise only on their account.

FINIS

INDEX

LIST OF SOURCES

SELECTED BIOGRAPHIES
The Life of Charlotte Bronte: Mrs E.C. Gaskell, Smith,
Elder & Co., 1857.
No. 318, Everyman's Library, J.M. Dent & Sons Ltd.,
1946.
The Penguin English Library, 1975.
Charlotte Bronte and Her Circle: Clement K. Shorter,
Hodder & Stoughton, 1896.
The Brontes, Life and Letters: (2 vols.), Clement K.
Shorter, Hodder & Stoughton, 1908.
Thornton and The Brontes: William Scruton, John Dale &
Co. Ltd., Bradford, 1898.
Pictures of the Past: Francis H. Grundy, Griffith & Farran,
1879.
The Brontes: Their Lives, Friendships and Correspondence
(4 vols.), Edited by T.J. Wise and J.A. Symington, The
Shakespeare Head Press, Oxford, 1932.
The Brontes' Web of Childhood: Fannie E. Ratchford,
Columbia University Press, New York, 1941.
Anne Bronte: Winifred Gerin, Thomas Nelson & Sons Ltd.,
1959.
Branwell Bronte: Winifred Gerin, Thomas Nelson & Sons
Ltd., 1961.
Charlotte Bronte: the Evolution of Genius, Winifred Gerin,
Oxford University Press, 1967.
Emily Bronte: Winifred Gerin, Oxford University Press,
1971.
A Man of Sorrow: The Life, Letters and Times of the Rev.
Patrick Bronte, John Lock and Canon W.T. Dixon,
Thomas Nelson & Sons Ltd., 1965.

TOPOGRAPHICAL
Haworth and The Brontes, W.R. Mitchell, Dalesman
Publishing Co. Ltd., 1969.
Half Inch Map Series, West Riding: John Bartholomew &
Son Ltd.

LIST OF SOURCES

PUBLISHED WORKS BY THE BRONTES

The Rev. Patrick Bronte
Cottage Poems, P.K. Holden, Halifax, 1811.
The Rural Minstrel (Poems), P.K. Holden, Halifax, 1813.
The Cottage in the Wood (A Romance), T. Inkersley,
    Bradford, 1815.
The Maid of Killarney (A Romance), Baldwin, Cradock &
    Joy, London, 1818.
The Phenomenon (A Poem), T. Inkersley, Bradford, 1824.

Anne Bronte
Contributions to Poems by Currer, Ellis and Acton Bell,
    Aylott & Jones, 1846.
Agnes Grey: T.C. Newby, 1847 and Smith, Elder & Co.,
    1850 and 1893.
The Tenant of Wildfell Hall: T.C. Newby, 1848 and Smith,
    Elder & Co., 1893.

Charlotte Bronte
Contributions to Poems by Currer, Ellis and Acton Bell,
    Aylott & Jones, 1846.
Jane Eyre: Smith, Elder & Co., 1847.
Shirley: Smith, Elder & Co., 1849.
Villette: Smith, Elder & Co., 1853.
Memoir to Emily in Selection of Ellis Bell's Poems.
Biographical Notes on Ellis and Acton Bell in Preface to
    later editions of Wuthering Heights and Agnes Grey.
The Professor: (published posthumously) Smith, Elder &
    Co., 1857.
Emma: a prose fragment (published posthumously) in
    The Cornhill Magazine, 1860.
The Spell (published posthumously) Oxford University
    Press.

Emily Jane Bronte
Contributions to Poems by Currer, Ellis and Acton Bell,
   Aylott & Jones, 1846.
Wuthering Heights: T.C. Newby, 1847 and Smith, Elder
   & Co., 1850 and 1893.
Selected Poems, edited by Charlotte Bronte.
The Complete Poems of Emily Jane Bronte, edited by
   C.W. Hatfield, Oxford University Press, 1952.

Patrick Branwell Bronte
Translations of the Odes of Horace (privately printed by
   John Drinkwater, 1910).